# Foodoodles

## FROM THE MUSEUM OF CULINARY HISTORY

For my sons, Max and Alex

# Foodoodles

## FROM THE MUSEUM OF CULINARY HISTORY

Cartoons & Commentaries by L. John Harris

*Foreword by Jeremiah Tower*

AN OAK ROCK BOOK
EL LEÓN LITERARY ARTS, BERKELEY, CALIFORNIA

*December 2012*

*to NSM*

*Team Crab*

*with love always!*

ISBN 978-0-9795285-6-9

Published by El León Literary Arts. El León is a private non-profit foundation established to extend the array of voices essential to a democracy's arts and education.

El León website: www.elleonliteraryarts.org

Distributed by Small Press Distribution, Inc.
800-869-7553
www.spdbooks.org
orders@spdbooks.org

Available on Amazon.com

Produced and designed by Oak Rock Books/Harris Publishing Co., Inc.
1563 Solano Ave, Suite 201, Berkeley, Ca., 94707
Email: harrispubco@gmail.com
Foodoodle website: www.foodoodles.com

A portion of the proceeds of sale to benefit the Berkeley Food and Housing Project
www.bfhp.org

# Menu

## Amuse-Bouche

## Hors d'Oeuvres

## PLATS PRINCIPAUX

*The Foodoodle Collection*

## Les Desserts

# Amuse-Bouche

## FOREWORD BY JEREMIAH TOWER

Can I prove that a society is at its healthiest when its culture of satire is fully developed, welcome and widely enjoyed? I cannot, but I do believe that to the extent a society takes loving potshots (itself a Foodoodle) at its closely-held shibboleths, the more that society can be seen to be still creatively developing, growing, and becoming ever more interesting.

In Latin "satire" stems from the root of a word meaning a "medley, dish of colorful fruits." What could be more relevant then, than satire for L. John Harris' *Foodoodles*? Latin satire is itself a Foodoodle!

The food revolution in the USA that started in the 1970's in California has gone the way the French political one did when the revolutionaries, bedecked in ribbons, rosettes, and peacock feathers, became more foppish than the aristocrats ever were. John, who I remember as a garlic promoter and cookbook publisher when I was the chef at Chez Panisse and later as chef and co-owner of the Santa Fe Bar & Grill in Berkeley, holds up his Foodoodle mirrors to the contemporary food scene to show, with all loving irony and sweet derision, how it can be improved. His tools are wit and parody, both well-tested satirical methods. He is a jester to the court of chefs and the foodies who follow their every whim.

Gilbert and Sullivan were master jesters:

*"I can set a braggart quailing with a quip,*
*The upstart I can wither with a whim.*

As was Lenny Bruce, who defined his times in direct proportion to the furor he created in those who believed in themselves without the slightest self doubt. San Francisco's Herb Caen supported Lenny when he was most attacked: "They call Lenny Bruce a sick comic, and sick he is. Sick of all the pretentious phoniness of a generation that makes his vicious humor meaningful. He is a rebel, but not without a cause, for there are shirts that need un-stuffing, egos that need deflating. [Oh, I see a soufflé Foodoodle!] Sometimes you feel guilty laughing at some of Lenny's mordant jabs, but that disappears a second later when your inner voice tells you with pleased surprise, 'but that's true.' "

The same way that *Foodoodles* is true. At every image I laugh, or take initial umbrage, or think he has gone too far, or not far enough, but I always end up loving them because they have spontaneity, candor, and are always 'true'.

I think that the English magazine *Punch* was the first to use the word "cartoon" for their satirical images. Choosing that "anarchic glove puppet, Mr. Punch," for their name, Punch was also a reference to a joke by one of its first editors that "punch is nothing without lemon."

All *Foodoodles'* punches are served with a loving dose of palatable sugar without losing any of their inspiringly educational acid edge. An edge that I believe goes to the heart of a contemporary American food scene that has truly lost its sense of humor, its ability to look in the mirror and see itself instead of what it self-importantly wants to see, as with the chef who recently boasted that he truly believed his main claim to fame was crushing garlic cloves with his fingers instead of a knife. Or, when I owned Stars in San Francisco, the number of times I had to explain to my chefs and cooks why I often laughed at some of their culinary heroes. Each of these kitchens had, I said, its own naked emperor. And the example I always gave was the time when at one of those restaurants the first course was a single scallop on a huge unadorned white plate with a tiny dollop of white sauce "on the side." One guest said, "What do we do with that, snort it?" He and I were the only ones at the table laughing. The rest of our group thought it sacrilege to make fun of the food of a famous chef. Even when it was funny.

If James Beard had been at the table he would have roared, perhaps not with laughter! Who else now but L. John Harris knows to catch the important frivolity and bubbly humor of James Beard now that he has been turned into a stuffy icon? Where else will you see Liz Windsor serving up Steak Diane? As so many, starting with Cicero, have said, inasmuch as we forget or do not know about the past, we are committed to repeating its sins. How many readers will know what a three-minute Steak Diane was before it was a princess in the hands of her mother-in-law? That it is a dish perfectly placed for a re-appearance in our contemporary, no-time society.

Perhaps my favorite laugh in *Foodoodles* is "Home Cooking." Anyone who has ever barbecued at home will get this one: the house being turned to cinders in a Weber grill. I think that *Foodoodles* will put some of the laughter back in the food business, thereby helping it re-discover some of its original creative dash. No need for a mirror: Just embrace the wit of *Foodoodles* and its wonderful cartoons.

**Jeremiah Tower**
**2009**

FISHER
13935 Sonoma Highway
Glen Ellen, CA 95442

January 22, 1990

Dear John:

First, let me thank you for coming up here, and for bringing that charming Michele with you. I was truly sorry to be more speechless than usual that day, especially for the lunch. But I assure you that the food, all of it very delicious indeed, served me well for several meals...

Now about the food doodles: they are amusing, light, and yet they say much more than they seem to. I hope you'll send me a lot more of them, as they appear, which I'm sure they will continue to do. I don't think your idea of my doing a foreword for a non-existent book is too good. You don't need any incentive at all.

Please get in touch with me whenever you're in this area. It's always fun to see you.

Excerpted letter from M.F.K. Fisher to author, used with permission. Reference in the first paragraph is to Michele Anna Jordan, the Sonoma County-based writer.

# Hors d'Oeuvres

*The duty of a good cuisinier is to transmit to the generations
who will replace him everything he has learned and experienced.*

— Fernand Point, *Ma Gastronomie,* 1974

## Curator's Note

† *The dagger symbol after a Foodoodle date indicates an entry
in An Anecdotal, Chronological Catalog of Foodoodles beginning
on page 129. To access this material, turn to the Catalog and
locate the corresponding Foodoodle date and page number.
Use the Catalog's thumbnail cartoons for easy reference.*

| JAMES'<br>BEARD | JULIA'S<br>CHILD | ALICE'S<br>WATER | JEREMIAH'S<br>TOWER |

From The Museum of Culinary History

(1990)[†]

Welcome to the Museum of Culinary History. MOCH* is a virtual culinary arts institution I discovered about 20 years ago while doodling in my journal. I had placed four American culinary legends on pedestals and titled the image "From the Museum of Culinary History."

I had not yet read A. J. Liebling's 1950's memoir, *Between Meals: An Appetite for Paris*, so I had no clue that, according to Liebling, the graphic arts were born during the Ice Age when men made "random designs in the snow with warm water." The first doodles! And I had no idea that my random museum food doodle would become an exhibit in a gastronomic *musée imaginaire*, or that I would someday open it to the public.

Now, as the self-appointed curator of MOCH, I offer my Foodoodle cartoon collection and commentaries with the hope that visitors to the museum will find amusement, if not instruction, in what I have seen and experienced as a veritable Forrest Gump in the trenches of an American gastronomic revolution that erupted in Berkeley in the 1970's, devoured California, and then ate its way across the U.S.

*Pronounced "mooch."

For visitors to the museum who may have missed it, what exactly was this so-called food revolution and how did it get started? I say so-called because although profoundly influenced by contemporary social and political movements, among them free speech, civil rights, back to the land, natural foods, women's lib and anti-war, it's important not to confuse them with our somewhat more genteel culinary uprising. Chefs' toques may have been rolling in the streets of Berkeley in the 1970's, not chefs' heads.

One recalls in history that after the aristocracy fell during the French Revolution, its chefs were released into the streets to make their own way. They created the restaurant as we know it today, and built a complex and hierarchical cuisine over the next century on the shoulders of genius chefs like Marie-Antoine Carême and Georges Auguste Escoffier. By an irony of historical perspective we can now see how the gastronomic forces unleashed in Berkeley, and then throughout the Bay Area and California, came to challenge in some key respects the very democratic advances in France that gave rise to the public expression of the restaurant (from the French *restaurer*, to restore) in the first place.

Food Revolution:
Off with His Toque!
(2008)

The French haute cuisine gold standard itself was now the target of a late 20th century food crusade that embraced, willy-nilly, France's lowest culinary expression, described by France's leading foodist of his day, Curnonsky, as "impromptu cooking" or "camper cuisine." Curnonsky, who was dubbed in 1927 the "Prince of Gastronomes," explained this simple ingredient-based cooking style in his *Traditional Recipes of the Provinces of France*, a book compiled from his writings after his death in 1956:

> It is done on a potluck basis, with whatever comes to hand... shrimps caught on the spot, fish from the nearby stream, milk from a farm close by, the best parts of a hare just decapitated by a speeding car, fruits from the hedgerows, vegetables "borrowed" from a farm when its owner isn't looking!... Like everything else in France they have that unique attraction... quality.

And that, in a nutshell, was our potluck revolution — gastronomy turned on its head. Young California foodists came to the table with offerings of an impromptu cuisine embracing quality ingredients as the flavorful stars of their dishes, shunning the highly-processed, over-packaged supermarket ingredients they had grown up with. Outshining the heavy sauces and overly elaborate presentations of high cuisine were vine-ripened heirloom tomatoes, young salad greens, seasonal vegetables and fruits, foraged wild mushrooms, free-range chickens, heritage pork and natural beef, all prepared and served simply. Like those avant-garde painters at the birth of our 20th century modern art who discovered that the vivid colors (and paints) they were using to depict their subjects *were* the subject of their work, California's artist chefs began serving forth the honest, unadorned and vivid taste of the food itself. "Fresh, local and seasonal" would become the California cuisine mantra.

Actual Heirloom Tomato
(2005)

By the 1980's some of the dishes being conceived in California kitchens were so impromptu that one wondered at times whether our new emperors of gastronomy were adequately dressed, let alone their salads and grills. This was now a haute (and expensive) camper cuisine and it spread like wildfire.

Call it what you will: California cuisine, new American cooking, market cooking, camper cuisine, impromptu cooking, haute home cooking, Slow Food, or as we present it at MOCH, Arts & Crafts cooking. The simple food style that evolved in California during the 70's, went national in the 80's and 90's, and was then challenged by new gastronomic complexities at century's end, is largely the focus of the Foodoodle Collection at my Museum of Culinary History.

The Revolution is over! Long live the revolution!

L. John Harris
**Curator, The Museum of Culinary History**
**2010**

# HEROES AND HEROINES OF THE REVOLUTION

*A*ll revolutions have heroes and heroines. My museum pays particular tribute to the giants of cuisine I have known and served with during my 40-year run as a dishwasher, waiter, shop clerk, cook, garlic activist, cookbook publisher, food doodler and food writer in and around the Gourmet Ghetto, Berkeley's culinary ground zero. The Ghetto was where mocha java (Peet's Coffee & Tea), French brie (The Cheese Board Collective) and local mesclun salads (Chez Panisse) came together to put my generation of foodists on America's gastronomic map.*

Alice and Jeremiah as Elizabeth David's Potted Rabbit and Pork
( 1986)[†]

Two subjects in my museum deserving of special attention are Alice Waters and Jeremiah Tower. Their collaboration at Chez Panisse in the 1970's is showcased at MOCH as our revolution's first skirmish, the birth of a California cuisine movement. Yet from the very beginning, theirs was an unlikely collaboration. Alice brought to the table a vision of the simple meals *à la Pagnol* she longed for after visits to Brittany and Provence in the 1960's, and Jeremiah arrived with the caviar dreams of Château d'Yquem and foie gras he grew up with in the 1950's. These extremes were simmered together in a melting pot of shared reverence for the French country and Mediterranean cooking presented in the books of the upper-crust British food authority, Elizabeth David.

* See "The Birth of a Ghetto" on page 81 for more of the story.

While the collaboration lasted, before Jeremiah moved on in the 80's to create his own legend cooking "new American cuisine" at his Stars restaurant in San Francisco, it could be argued that Waters and Tower were the most innovative culinary arts duo since Auguste Escoffier and César Ritz reinvented modern cuisine and dining in the late 19th century.

Unlike Escoffier and Ritz, however, who apparently worked happily together for many years, the stormy liaison of Waters, the good little girl, and Tower, the big bad boy, disintegrated rather abruptly. I am reminded of transformative yet doomed duos in other historical contexts: Chancellor Bismarck and Kaiser Wilhelm II in Germany come to mind, and of course Martin and Lewis in Hollywood.

In Tower's 2003 memoir, *California Dish*, he compares his collaboration with Alice Waters to the sparring French surrealist icons, his Guillaume Apollinaire (artist) to her Andre Breton (impresario). I understand his rationale: He was the chef and Alice wasn't. But the early drama at Chez Panisse, staged in a culinary bohemianism where art, love, politics and duck confit made claim to moral and aesthetic equivalence, was more theater of the absurd than surrealism. Waters and Tower were characters only a Eugène Ionesco could imagine. But let's not quibble over art labels. The fact remains that in its prime, the team of Waters and Tower changed the course of American gastronomy, and, on a somewhat lesser note, my own Gumpian career path.*

* Full disclosure: Beyond some informal training and time served in the early 70's in a cafe kitchen and then operating a professional recipe testing kitchen at Aris Books in the 1980's, I can't claim to have been possessed with the combination of talent, ambition and grit it takes to be a cook on the line, let alone a chef de cuisine. There were, however, many ways to support the revolution. In military parlance, while I seldom fought with boots on the ground, I racked up years of service in KP, communications and intelligence.

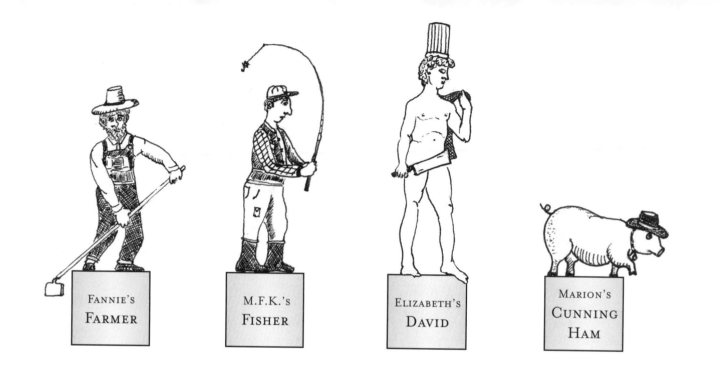

From the Museum of Culinary History — Literary Heroes
(2008)

MOCH also serves to highlight the literary heroes — the food writers, essayists and cookbook authors — who told my generation of foodists in words and recipes what dishes to eat, how to prepare them and the cultural or personal stories behind each one. These legends were the gods of a new generation of food writers.

The Galloping Gourmet
GRAHAM KERR
1934 –

The French Chef
JULIA CHILD
1912 – 2004

Emeril Live
EMERIL LAGASSE
1959 –

Iron Chef Mario
MARIO BATALI
1960 –

Four Celebrity Chefs on TV
(2009)[†]

If the visitor to MOCH suspects that my museum's exhibits are antiquarian, looking backward perhaps too fondly to Berkeley's golden gastronomical moment, they would be mistaken. Although my generation of accidental foodists may be passing the baton to a new avant-garde, our story remains relevant as it reflects on and influences the exciting new food trends and movements of the day, from haute test-tube gastronomy to roving twittering foodiemobiles.

Worthy of its own wing in my museum is the story of television's effect on gastronomy and vice versa. MOCH boldly examines the proliferation of competitive cooking programs on channels like the Food Network, Bravo and PBS, a subset of sports broadcasting, in particular boxing and wrestling, overlaid with game-show formats and the heavily packaged reality TV genre.

Being a graduate of Berkeley's anti-war/pro-food decade of the 70's, I prefer my televised cooking non-violent. Humor works, however. I remember when Martin Yan's TV show, "Yan Can Cook," first aired in the Bay Area in the 1980's. He played the charming culinary clown. Before him was the wonderful English cooking show host, Graham Kerr. Although not as great a cook as he was a drinker, he sure knew how to serve up ham and corn! And, of course, Julia Child cracked us up on TV with her natural goofiness long before she became a pop culture icon. Yes, let's have more food humor on TV, and food politics, too. "Make Food Not War!" is the name of my own stand-up cooking show, presented exclusively at the Museum of Culinary History. Check our website for schedules.

Top, Bottom and Middle Chef
(2009)

# DOODLING BEFORE FOODOODLES

Sloop a l'Oignon
(1985)

*R*evolutions, even food revolutions, have unintended consequences, cultural and personal. If the decade of the 1970's had been a glorious potluck free-for-all, in the 80's my comrades and I got down to some serious business, and serious business can mean trouble!

I had launched a cookbook publishing venture in 1981, Aris Books, to showcase some of the food talent emerging in the Bay Area. But like those doodling Ice Age artists A.J. Liebling writes about, with saber-toothed tigers breathing down their necks, I suddenly had bankers and investors breathing down mine. Cookbook publishing turned out to be anything but a *pique-nique*.

Aris did manage some notable successes thanks to the Bay Area legends we were lucky enough to publish, among them goat-cheese pioneer Laura Chenel; the feisty and inspirational Breton cook, Josephine Araldo; chef/fishmonger to the stars, Paul Johnson; and prose master M.F.K. Fisher. But by the end of the decade our tasteful, literary cookbooks were struggling against a flood of celebrity chef "food porn," the popular coffee table photo cookbooks made possible by cheap color printing technology emerging in Asia. Aris' goose was getting cooked!

Until the opportunity arose to sell Aris Books to Boston's Addison-Wesley in 1990, I found relief from business worries while drawing food toons I titled with Frenchified puns and double entendres in my journal books. I was back, at least while doodling, in the carefree bohemian demimonde of my student days.

I remember the night when the first official Foodoodle emerged, a little sail boat shaped like an onion and with a chef at the tiller.

Hero on a Flying T-bone
(1970)

Unofficially the food doodling began during my years in U.C. Berkeley's art department. Food imagery often appeared in my drawings and collages, and in the black cloth-bound journal books that were *de rigueur* in my crowd of poets, artists and Anais Nin-style diarists. One drawing from that period features an embedded T-bone steak. I don't know why exactly but I have always loved drawing steaks, especially bone-in steaks, maybe because I was better at drawing them than, say, people. I don't think there is anything Freudian in my graphic attachment to beefsteak. Sometimes a T-bone is just a T-bone.

It can also be noted that the hero in this drawing has the same cartoonish quality as some of the Foodoodle characters that would appear decades down the road, as if these entities were engineered into my hand. The nature of my iconographic style is not something I think much about at this point. Though as a child, and later as an art student, I dearly wished I could draw better, I console myself with a paraphrase of Picasso's famous line about seeking vs. finding in the arts: Style is not sought, it's found. I found mine in my Foodoodles!

In the decade of the 1980's, with California's haute camper cuisine aesthetic well established, our food revolution, labeled now by the media the "new American cooking," headed east, buoyed by a national economic surge. While innovative young chefs were portrayed in the food press as culinary artists, the art media were identifying young artists who were finding fresh opportunities with food as a fine arts medium.* Here's what a writer who called herself Susie Creamcheese wrote about food art in a small (2" x 4") Bay Area art magazine, *Kajun Call*, in the summer of 1981:

> *American restaurant and art critics point to Julia Child making a jelly roll look like a mushroom-covered log on nationwide TV as the impetus for the food art of the Eighties.*

The publisher of this underground zine, the graphic artist Jeanne Jambu was the designer of most of the early books I published at Aris Books. She knew about my art school background and asked me to contribute to a forthcoming issue of *Kajun Call* titled "Eat Art."** I knew exactly what to do.

---

\* Food artists today are tying political/environmental/social food issues together with the inherent performance and art elements of food culture and cooking. At the Whitney Museum in New York, artist Corin Hewitt presented "Seed Stage" in 2008, turning an area of the museum into a studio where the artist carried on daily activities such as cooking and eating, even growing vegetables and canning. And more recently, a group of Chez Panisse cooks and staff began operating what they call OPENrestaurant to experiment with the "codes and architecture" of restaurants in front of live audiences at a variety of public venues.

\*\* The title of this issue of *Kajun Call* was perhaps influenced by the Eat Art events produced in Europe in the 1960's by the artist Daniel Spoerri. For more on Spoerri's food art, see note, page 133.

Piecasso
(2009)†

I had always wondered, after taking an undergraduate art history survey of the work of Picasso, what his awkward-looking right arm and curled fist had been holding in the 1906 *Self Portrait with Palette*. Although my professor and his textbooks did not address this art historical puzzle, it was obvious to me that something had been painted out of the original composition. But what? I could visualize paint brushes or a small dog, but came up with another idea — a pie.

I submitted my collage titled "Eat Your Art Out, Piecasso" with the artist's signature enlarged at the bottom, doctored by inserting an "e" I had drawn. I hoped that it would integrate seamlessly into the iconic signature. The collage and signature appeared in that summer issue of *Kajun Call*.

As the decade of the 80's came to a close, and with pressures mounting at Aris, it appeared that my lingering "fine art" impulses had become no more than escapist hobbying. But when the Bay Area magazines *Berkeley Insider* and *Bay Food* offered me a monthly byline, "Foodoodles," my foodist doodles became more than random Ice Age designs in the snow.

# WHAT KIND OF ART IS FOOD?

*T*he food revolution swept through my life like a tsunami. When the storm had passed, so had my plans for being a painter, or a poet, or an actor. I never believed that I was abandoning dreams of art for food, merely opting for one art form, albeit a special one, over others — the Culinary Arts. I was not alone as many of my foodist comrades had come to Berkeley with ambitions unrelated to gastronomy. We were bohemian aesthetes and autodidacts who discovered a passion for the profession of food. I don't think most of us even knew what the word *gastronomy* really meant. It sounded more like a medical term, something that doctors do inside the gastrointestinal tract, than what food artists were doing in Berkeley's Gourmet Ghetto.

But the question is begged, what kind of art *is* food? MOCH is built on the premise that cuisine can achieve a high level of art in the hands of brilliant cooks and those who assist and supply them. Is this merely a foodie conceit? Or a conspiracy perpetrated by the gastro-industrial complex to sell more pots and pans, magazine subscriptions and dream-kitchen makeovers? When one's lived in Berkeley for more than 40 years, one considers these questions.

It's true that a fabulous Blanquette de Veau, such as the one I enjoyed recently in Paris, is not art in the same way that a painting by Claude Monet is art. For one thing the Monet can hang on its museum wall indefinitely, if properly preserved, whereas an ephemeral Blanquette rots away before it can make it up the museum's steps, through the doors and onto a pedestal.

Even the arts of dance, music and theater can be nominally preserved through audio or visual recordings, notwithstanding the late Merce Cunningham's lament about the dance, reported in the *New York Times* (July 28, 2009) just after his death: "It gives you nothing back… no paintings to show on walls… no poems to be printed and sold… nothing but that single fleeting moment when you feel alive." Mr. Cunningham might just as well have been talking about chefs and the art of cuisine.

Blanquette de Veau
(2009)

The philosopher of art, Professor Denis Dutton, in his 2009 book *The Art Instinct*, argues that true art, unlike craft, and he defines cooking as craft,* has an element of unpredictability. According to Dutton, the artist, unlike the chef who has a very clear idea of the dish he is cooking, never knows in advance what the final work will turn out to be — no recipes allowed and no painting by the numbers. Art unfolds like a mystery and the artist is just as surprised by the final product as the viewer. Or, as Dutton puts it, "… creative artists strictly speaking never know what they're doing." Voila! That's me in the kitchen: I don't use recipes, the results are unpredictable and, "strictly speaking," I never know what I'm doing. No wonder my dinner guests call me a true artist in the kitchen.

Granted, I'm no philosopher of art. I surmise that Professor Dutton is no foodie. Art vs. craft, artist vs. chef — none of these distinctions matters at my Museum of Culinary History, where food is art and art is food and a Blanquette de Veau can be a masterpiece.

* Anthony Bourdain agrees. In his tell-all memoir, *Kitchen Confidential* (2000), he says "Cooking is a craft, I like to think, and a good cook is a craftsman — not an artist." Maybe Bourdain takes this position because he is just a "good cook." In other words, his art is in spilling the beans, not cooking them.

# CULINARY REVOLUTION 101

*I* think I first truly understood the revolution and what had happened in California when I came across Jean-François Revel's 1981 book, *Culture & Cuisine*. In it he identifies a pattern in Western gastronomy:

*Periodically in the course of this history we see a return to the natural product being preached as a reaction against an excessively heavy and complicated cuisine.*

Of course Revel is talking about a much more global phenomenon than what was taking place in our little foodist ghetto in North Berkeley. Yet that is exactly what was being played out within our community of culinary aesthetes — a pendulum swing away from the gastronomic complexity of technique-centered haute cuisine cooking, to ingredient-based simplicity. It helped that our revolutionary cooks were mostly amateurs. It's easier to simplify culinary complexity when you haven't been formally trained in it.

Operating on its own terms, only vaguely aware of the related swing of France's Nouvelle cuisine,* a radical, almost instinctive credo began to emerge from Berkeley's kitchen brigades: use local, fresh, seasonal ingredients. They were harvested from our very own terroirs of Napa and Sonoma, Mendocino and Monterey, Marin and Contra Costa. Hyped-up media-flaunted slogans and code words — organic, sustainable, artisanal, range-fed, free-range, head-to-tail, farm-to-table, farm-raised, pasture-raised, line-caught, biodynamic, locavore, slow, hand-crafted and, most recently noted, wild-crafted — were still decades away.

---

* Nouvelle cuisine was actually not so new, as Revel's observation would explain. The star chefs who launched the French movement in the 1960's, chef/graduates of Fernand Point's legendary restaurant La Pyramide near Lyons (Paul Bocuse, Jean and Pierre Troisgros and Roger Vergé among others), made headlines with their efforts to simplify and lighten the late 19th century grand cuisine of Escoffier. Yet Escoffier himself had done the same for Carême's early 19th century cuisine which itself had promoted fresh vegetables and simplified sauces. It's comparable to the swings in the fashion world where what is old invariably becomes *nouvelle* again.

The Bay Area was re-discovered as a gastronomic gold mine of almost mythical richness, our cities surrounded by bountiful ranch and farmlands. Not since the gold rush would greater San Francisco be credited with so much natural wealth. Even Berkeley had been built on farm land and the corny advertising slogan for Berkeley's venerable local dairy, Berkeley Farms, was, we came to understand, actually true: "Cows in Berkeley? Moo!"

Once Upon a Time When All Chickens Were Range Fed
(1986)

My own immersion in Berkeley's ingredio-centricity took the form of an obsession with just one ingredient — garlic.* The food revolution was for me, at least in the 1970's, a garlic revolution. It was while waiting tables and eating at Chez Panisse during its hectic and heady opening days in 1971 that I began thinking about humble garlic as the under-appreciated *je ne sais quoi* of the world's great cooking. There was no avoiding this conclusion at Provence-inspired Chez Panisse. The aioli was flowing! I think it was James Beard who first referred to garlic as the base note in cooking, the tuba in cuisine's symphony orchestra. I concluded, after extensive research, that this much-maligned gastronomic hero, and perhaps the world's funniest and most subversive food, was indeed worthy of its very own treatise.

* I was not the only writer or cook to become single-ingredient-obsessed, and I sought out kindred spirits to work with me at Aris Books. Among them: Isaac Cronin (squid); Bruce Cost (ginger); Laura Chenel (goat cheese); Georgeanne Brennan (hot peppers); Linda Burum (Asian noodles); Maggie Klein (olive oil); Tim Castle (coffee); Marti Sousanis (filo); Michele Anna Jordan (mustard). The single-subject cookbook had become an essential format for adventurous, flavor-starved cooks.

While working on *The Book of Garlic*, I spent considerable time in the town of Gilroy, California, one of the largest centers of garlic farming and processing in the world. Driving south from San Francisco, you could smell Gilroy starting in San Jose! It was eye (and nostril) opening to discover that Gilroy's abundance of the "stinking rose"* was not directed at the fresh produce market but, rather, used primarily as raw material for its huge, and pungent, dehydration factories producing garlic salts, powders, chips and related fodder for commercial products like ketchup, bottled salad dressings and pet food.

One of the most important lessons I learned from my interviews with garlic farmers and processors in Gilroy was that dogs and cats, according to industry studies, prefer their canned meat and fish meals laced with dehydrated garlic.

Our garlic revolution had a profound impact on Gilroy. I had worked with Chez Panisse to develop their first annual Bastille Day Garlic Festival in 1975, and so I was invited by the town fathers of Gilroy to help them promote their own festival in 1978, the now world-famous Gilroy Garlic Festival. Conservative, garlic-processing Gilroy had discovered during those early years of the revolution, as had Berkeley's radical foodists earlier on, that people preferred their meals with large doses of *fresh* garlic.

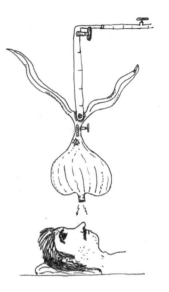

Provençal Aroma Therapy
(1989)[†]

* "Stinking rose" is a term I coined while researching *The Book of Garlic*, the translation of a Roman slang expression for garlic, "fetid rose." Following the publication of the book in 1974, the garlic fan club, Lovers of the Stinking Rose (LSR), was launched and the term became quite popular. A San Francisco restaurateur took the name for his new restaurant, The Stinking Rose, which opened in 1991 and has become a small chain. (There is no relationship between the restaurant or the food served there to Lovers of the Stinking Rose, or anyone associated with the club, past or present.)

Inevitably, ingredient-forward art cooking, unrestrained by the disciplined rigidities of old-world kitchens, got a little out of hand with fads and fashions. The garlic frenzy of the 70's was followed in the 80's by the baby vegetable craze and all the fuss about perfect little lettuces. The food media loved the excesses that pushed California cuisine to the edge of caricature.

I was actually OK with the little vegetables — for me, a little vegetable goes a long way. But what I didn't understand, I confess, were the smaller protein portions served with the tiny vegetables. Where were the big steaks I had learned to love (and draw) growing up in Los Angeles? Was it simply a matter of scale, or were our anti-meat politics starting to show?

Adding insult to injury were the preciously artsy slice-and-fan and slice-and-stack plating arrangements that emerged and linger on. Do we really need help from chefs, as if we were children, cutting our meat into little pieces? And do plates piled high with decorative layers of food increase our eating pleasure or merely induce sensations of culinary vertigo?

Another annoyance that grew out of our obsession with top-notch local ingredients was the absurd compulsion to rename classic European dishes on our simple food menus with overly-detailed, supplier-branded descriptions. Isn't "Round of grass-fed Happy Cow beef, braised in Fussy Vineyards pinot noir, with organic Cookie Cutter Farms baby carrots and pearl onions," in fact, Boeuf Bourguignon? Our menus began to read more like shopping lists than that medley of classic, named dishes that evoked cherished taste memories on menus past.

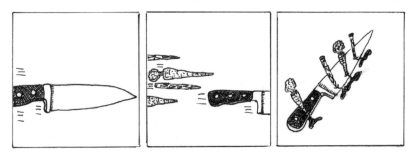

Revenge of the Baby Vegetables
(1992)

And what about the overwrought prose of certain food writers, especially some of the restaurant critics? Who are they, anyway, and what are their qualifications, literary or culinary? Is it true that restaurant criticism emerged way back when, out of the womens' and sports pages of newspapers? According to *San Francisco Chronicle* columnist, the late, great, Charles McCabe, during slow news days in the sports world, or when local game match-ups failed to inspire, the writers would go out for elaborate meals at fancy restaurants and then write about them. I suppose the truly outstanding meals were "home runs" and "touchdowns" and the bad ones "strikeouts" and "fumbles."

Food Critics
(1991)

Pet peeves aside, America's bottom-up simple-food revolution had prevailed. Our best wines, breads, cheeses, vegetables and meats now compared favorably with or even surpassed those from France, and young chefs indoctrinated with California cuisine's powerful ethic were pouring out of our culinary academies like sea salt.

Incredibly, France, where we first fell in love with food, was, at century's end (according to some observers), in gastronomical decline. (See Michael Steinberger's 2009 *Au Revoir to All That: Food, Wine, and the End of France* for the full picture.) Coming up fast from behind was Italy's Slow Food movement launched in the 1980's. And rubbing raw garlic into France's open wound was the amazing gastronomic rise of Spain in the 1990's with its Andalusian (sherry) bar food aesthetic (tapas) and an ultra complex Molecular Gastronomy that put haute cuisine in the hands of haute technology. The pendulum had swung again.

THE GLUTTON
*Pre–16th Century*

THE GASTRONOME
*16th–19th Century*

THE GOURMET
*20th Century*

THE GASTRONAUT
*21st Century and Beyond*

From the Museum of Culinary History — Evolving Types
(1990)[†]

# Gastronomic Swing Time

As I began to curate the Foodoodle Collection for MOCH, and reflect on my history, personal and professional which brought me to this project, I approached Charlie Perry, co-founder of the Culinary Historians of Southern California and a comrade in arms during the garlic revolution,* for a status check on our simple-food revolution. Charlie offered a clever twist on Jean-François Revel's earlier observations (see page 27) on gastronomy's pendulum swings:

> *When people can afford to have rich, complex dishes, they revel in them — until they become bored, and then they rediscover the virtues of simplicity, preferably an expensive sort of simplicity.*

Yes, an expensive sort of simplicity! It's a paradox of our culinary reform movement very similar to that of the design reform movement of the late 19th century — Arts and Crafts — when artisan-made handicrafts, furniture and textiles were unaffordable by all but the well-to-do. The revolutionary food we have been making since the 1970's may be simple, but it isn't really affordable by "simple" people.

Maybe that's why many American foodies appear to be getting bored with our revolution's simple food cuisine. Marketing food that is sustainable, hand-crafted and organic may justify a premium price to be sure, but if the price is sky high, then perhaps the cuisine should be more haute than simple. Do the trendy gastronauts of the new Molecular Gastronomy, led by Chef Ferran Adrià's *nueva cocina* gang at elBulli in Spain, with their space-age cooking technologies, their foams, gels and gums, their syringes, test tubes and *sous vide* machines, represent a pendulum swing back to a technique-centered complexity? Is gastronomy turning on its head once again, from bottom-up to top-down?

---

* Charlie presided over the Southern California chapter of Lovers of the Stinking Rose in the 1970's and 1980's and marched alongside a garlic-themed float at annual Pasadena Doo Dah Parades, a spoof of the Rose Bowl Parade.

To help address these questions I needed to get a better taste of the popular genre of "edge cuisine," as Michael Ruhlman calls the Molecular Gastronomy movement in his 2006 book *The Reach of a Chef*: "… cooking in which the method over-shadowed the food itself, in which classic dishes were so deconstructed they didn't look like anything you could ever recognize." I had spent almost four decades immersed in gastronomic simplicity and needed a good dose of this new complexity.

I chose Daniel Patterson's Coi in San Francisco as the movement's most radical local showcase, though it might be more accurate to group Patterson with the more moderate American "meta-" or "trans-" molecular chefs who, we are told, combine "organic purity and synthetic preparation and structure."* Whatever *that* means! As with all avant-garde art movements, the nuanced labels keep piling up — think cubism to analytical cubism to synthetic cubism.

My interest in Patterson, formerly of the restaurants Babette's, Elizabeth Daniels and Frisson, was sparked in 2005 after he had thrown down a gastronomic gauntlet in a *New York Times Magazine* article titled "To the Moon, Alice?" In the piece, he bravely described his frustration with the admittedly delicious but unimaginative "home cooking" of the Chez Panisse school of California cuisine that appeared to him to be constraining creativity in professional kitchens.

Patterson's article was blasted by elements within the food community. His supporters brought up the old specter of an embedded Bay Area food mafia operating out of the Church of California Cuisine, Chez Panisse, defending it against outright sacrilege or even the hint of gastronomical incorrectness. I can't confirm the mafia claim, though I can imagine a conspiratorial gathering of the restaurant's founding cabal of loyalists and soldiers which might include Marion "Ma Baker" Cunningham, Greil "Rock Man" Marcus, Tom "the Flick" Luddy and members of the Shere family. Pouring the wine in a back room of Tommaso's Restaurant, his hangout in San Francisco's North Beach, would be none other than Francis Ford "the Godfather" Coppola. And presiding over Chez Panisse's notorious "board" would be the boss of all bosses herself, Alice "Baby Carrots" Waters, plotting the gang's next restaurant hit.

* From Jerry Weinberger's article "America's Food Revolution" in *City Journal* (Summer 2009).

But let's get back to curatorial business! Though one could argue Patterson's premise, and even question his motives, he survived the fury. To his credit, Patterson answered back with the opening of Coi in 2006. Putting his money where his mouth was, Patterson's ambitious menu tested and tasted the boundaries of cuisine. My meal in the early spring of 2009 was fascinating to be sure. A whimsical art happening on tiny plates, including deep-fried gelatinized chicken bouillon ("fried chicken") and freeze-dried butter-milk powder ("snow flakes") for a winter/spring pea soup.

I left Coi amused and dazzled by the sheer technical display. This was gastronomic territory light years away from Webster's definition of a meal: "The portion of food taken at a particular time to satisfy appetite." But was Patterson's food edge cuisine or over-the-edge cuisine?

And One Giant Leap for Gastronomy
(2009)

On my way home I compared the dishes I had at Coi to one I remembered at Chez Panisse a few months earlier: Chef Jean-Pierre Moullé's ragout of lingcod and American lobster. The rich, golden broth was so clear that the perfect little chunks of lobster and lingcod appeared to swim about like exotic miniature fish in an aquarium. And you could almost count the individual flecks of thyme suspended in a liquid that tasted of the sea, sweet and clean. This was simple food, to be sure, yet subtly transcendent. Not at all the surreal distortions of Patterson's expressionism, Moullé's naturalistic dish was more the work of a magical realism.

Later that night, as I prepared for bed, my thoughts returned to Daniel Patterson's astonishing technical transformations. Scary images of those "man-made" green wafers from the 1970's cult sci-fi film, *Soylent Green*, haunted my overactive culinary imagination.

# Simultaneous Culinary Oscillation

*I*f we have now competitive trends in a post-revolutionary cuisine that pits high-tech complexity against hand-made simplicity, is a showdown looming? After all, food war, like all war, has winners and losers. Historian Paul Freedman, in the 2009 anthology *Food: The History of Taste*, appears to think not:

> *The oscillation between magnificence and simplicity, between artifice and authenticity, is particularly typical of the current culinary scene, where the two contradictory trends flourish simultaneously rather than one era succeeding another.*

A flourishing simultaneous culinary oscillation! Perhaps. The late French filmmaker, Jean Renoir, presents a less sanguine perspective regarding the tensions between "artifice and authenticity," the technical and the natural, in the arts. During a discussion* of the effects of emerging technologies on the cinema, Renoir states:

> *I wonder if our technical advances don't simply herald complete decadence... Progress works against art and artistic expression.*

Only the artist, Renoir continues, whether in cinema, fine art or cuisine, is able to overcome, to humanize, the inevitable tyranny of technique. At the end of the interview, Renoir underscores his point with an example from the culinary arts:

> *A true chef doesn't use a technique, he works instinctively, using his senses.*

Cuisine is inherently conservative and slow to change and at MOCH we make no predictions about its future. We will follow the pendulum swings and oscillations wherever they take us and, while the story of the American food revolution is still being written, offer our Foodoodle Collection for the record.

* From Jacques Rivette's 1975 film *Jean Renoir et son Art*, reproduced for the Criterion Collection.

# PLATS PRINCIPAUX

## THE FOODOODLE COLLECTION

The history of Gastronomy is that of manners, if not of morals;
and the learned are aware that its literature is both instructive and amusing;
for it is replete with curious traits of character and comparative views of society
at different periods, as well as with striking anecdotes of remarkable men and
women whose destinies have been strangely influenced by their epicurean tastes
and habits. Let it, moreover, be remembered, that a tone of mock seriousness
or careless gaiety does not necessarily imply the absence of sound reflection.

— Abraham Hayward, *The Art of Dining; or, Gastronomy and Gastronomers*, 1852

# Food History & Lore

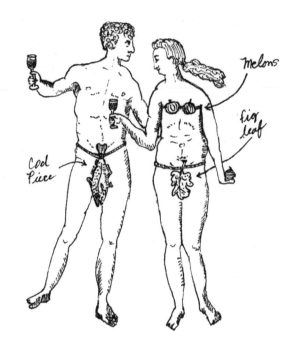

Melons

fig
leaf

Cod
Piece

When Food Was Underwear
(2008)[†]

# THE ART OF GASTRONOMY
# AND THE GASTRONOMY OF ART

*T*he legendary gastronome Jean-Anthelm Brillat-Savarin gave us one of the most quoted, often misquoted, and perhaps over-quoted assertions in the literature of gastronomy in his early 19th century classic, *The Physiology of Taste*: "Tell me what you eat and I shall tell you what you are." At MOCH we speculate on what Brillat-Savarin might have said if he had been an artist, not a writer: "Show me what you eat and I shall show you what you are."

Can there be a gastronomy of art, cuisine's reflection in the mirror of art history and its classic two-dimensional formats: portraiture, the human body, landscape and still life?* We answer, "Yes, as long as there is food on the plate and people to eat it, there is still life."

We also must acknowledge that at the heart of Western gastronomy is an anthropocentric bias that claims dominion of the planet for man, including, as cataloged in *Genesis*, the "trees bearing fruit," "the winged birds" and "sea monsters," and "all that lives and moves upon the earth." Though most world religions give us permission to be the planet's managing consumers, they go to great lengths to explain, albeit cryptically, the rules. For example,

* Three-dimensional art formats such as sculpture and architecture can also be "gastronomized," and we note the edible and inedible installations of the food art movement of the 1960's to 1980's and its recent re-emergence. (See footnote, page 23.)

CURATOR'S NOTE

*In this wing at MOCH we focus on the art and lore of gastronomy in the historical context of the West. The following exhibits explore the nourishment of human beings and reflect on the interplay of cuisine and culture. It is cold curatorial fact, however, that culinary historians cannot replicate the actual meals eaten in the distant past and are therefore limited to graphic and literary representations. Although one can examine well-preserved cooking and eating implements from the earliest human societies, and explore written recipes that date back to the Romans, we can never, aside from the expert approximations of forensic culinarians, taste what the ancients tasted or smell what they smelled — a good thing, perhaps, in many cases. The scenes and characters from art history and popular gastronomical lore on display in the historical wing at MOCH must suffice to represent our rich gastronomic heritage and set the stage for the museum's exhibits that make up the remainder of the Foodoodle Collection.*

eat fish on Friday if you are Catholic, but if Jewish, only eat fish with scales, and never shellfish; if Muslim and Jewish, do not eat pork or combine the acceptable meats (beef, lamb, goat, poultry, etc.) with dairy in the same meal; but if not Jewish, Muslim or Seventh-Day Adventist, pork may be eaten, even braised in milk and herbs (with delicious results).

Some religious groups discourage animal consumption altogether, in particular Hindus, Buddhists and Jains. Extreme or "strict" vegetarians known as vegans, though technically not a religion, consume no animals or animal by-products, including cheese, eggs and milk. Honey, however, is acceptable to some vegans, much to the dismay of others, adding to the mystery of our fickle gastronomical creation.

Despite the mixed messages regarding what's on the plate, all religions appear to agree in principle that people should not eat each other. But even here there are exceptions: The cannibals of the Aghori Hindu sect in India are one well-documented example.

The Museum of Culinary History examines gastronomy's anthropocentrism, its contradictions and consequences. From earth's ecocentric point of view, to which we are increasingly sensitive, and that of the hungry creatures who share with humans the planet's resources, man himself may be the ultimate foodie treat.

The First Edible School Yard

(2009)

Mummy's Preserves
(1991)

Tales of Old Rome:
When Food First Became Entertainment
(2008)

To the amazement of the other cooks the young Arthur pulled the chef's knife out of the butcher block with ease.

Arthurian Legend: The Knife in the Butcher Block
(2008)[†]

Medieval Origins of the Chef's Toque
(1992)

Botticelli's Cup of Tea
(2008)[†]

Typical Punishment for a
15th Century Chef Caught Pilfering
(2008)[†]

Executive Chef Quixote and Sous Chef Panza
(2009)[†]

His Last Supper
(2008)[†]

Soup Peddler in
Warsaw, circa 1895

Origins of the Term "Borscht Belt"
(2008)[†]

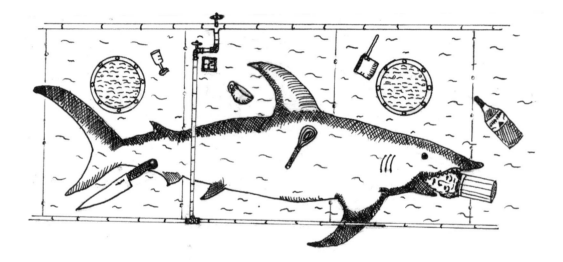

Last Meal Aboard the Titanic
(2008)

Salvador Deli

(2009)<sup>†</sup>

James Beard at the Gilroy Garlic Festival
(2008)[†]

*Liz Windsor (formerly Queen Elizabeth II) demonstrates a French classic and Royal Family favorite: Steak Diane*

BBC TV's New Cooking Host

(2008)

Harvesting Thyme          Cooking with Thyme          Serving Thyme

Got Thyme? Martha Does!
(2008)

# Chefs & the Restaurant Trade

Two Performance Artists
(1987)

# DINNER THEATER

*P*rior to the transformation of the culinary arts into a branch of the performing arts in the second half of the 20th century, chefs were artists in their ateliers, working their magic behind closed doors, out of public view. There was something hermetic and mysterious about the art of cuisine, even religious. Chefs were the high priests of gastronomy and their art was praised, at its best, as heavenly and revelatory. Great restaurants were described as temples and shrines of gastronomy and diners experienced ecstacies and epiphanies.

Old-school chefs/artists/priests did emerge from their sacred kitchens from time to time to greet customers or perform tableside. They were, according to Robert Courtine in his splendid *The Hundred Glories of French Cooking* (1973):

> *... always ready to indulge in anything a little showy, a little excessive, always inclined to throw in a little pinch of arrogance and self-display.*

Today chefs are less priests than entertainers, performing now in open kitchens and on television. Their chef's whites are up-fashion "chef wear" modeled in glossy trade catalogs and on the Internet. The universally identifiable chef's toque, whether the floppy or tall variety, borrowed from the style of head gear worn by 16th century magistrates and tradesmen, is now being replaced, post-revolution, by hip bandanas and baseball caps, at least on popular television cooking shows. But no matter how they are dressed, chefs today, as if they were soldiers just back from a war with ribbons on their chests, are increasingly full of themselves, puffed up and putting on a show. As Michael Ruhlman observes in his *The Soul of a Chef* (2000):

> *The chefs at the CIA were actual chefs, but they were also playing at being chefs, projecting their chefness... So what I was seeing was the professional chef almost in caricature.*

Describing Chef Ferran Adrià and his role at his monumental elBulli in Spain, the restaurant where Molecular Gastronomy found its first major platform, artist Richard Hamilton writes in the 2008 book *Food for thought, Thought for food*:

> *While the debate on the question of Ferran's classification as an artist unfolds, it becomes clear that elBulli is a troupe of players... writing the scripts and staging the event superbly, in a theatre of its own making.*

While chefs are obviously the celebrity players in gastronomy's new dinner theater, they are not, as Richard Hamilton points out, alone on stage. There are a variety of supporting characters in a restaurant troupe that are critical for the show's success and who deserve credit in their own right. I have a particular interest in the role of the servers or waitstaff, formerly known as waiters and waitresses. Perhaps because I have been one, I know first hand the difficult and essential role that they play in a successful dinner theater experience. Servers can make or break a production and often represent the highlight of a meal, like brilliant character actors with small juicy parts that upstage the lead.

I was reminded of this point at the upstairs Café at Chez Panisse a few years ago. My pompous server, a stocky fellow in his early 40's, responded to my request for 'lamb, medium rare' with the single most outrageous line (though not the rudest) I've ever received at table. "I'm sorry," he offered in an officious tone, "but our chef does not solicit calibration preferences." It took me a moment to figure it out, and when I did, I didn't know whether to punch the guy in the nose or fall off my chair laughing.

I don't remember the details of the food that night — how could I? But I won't forget the server! He was the highlight of the evening, and as it turns out, he was, in fact, an out-of-work actor. I later met him through mutual friends at a dinner party and shared my memory of his wonderful retort. He chuckled. "You know," he said a bit defensively, "that was just my Chez Panisse performance style."

I ran into him yet again the following year serving at a new Oakland restaurant and his performance style had changed dramatically. He had become pleasant and a little unsure of himself, exactly, and appropriately, like the food he was now serving. I preferred his bravura role at the Chez Panisse Café, but in today's competitive world of dinner theater, unless you are a headliner you accept the roles that come your way.

This Special "Chef's Special" Is Served with the Special Chef
(2009)

Batterie de Cuisine

(1991)

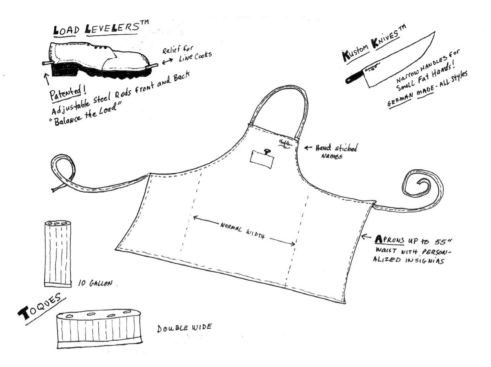

LOAD LEVELERS™

Relief for
Line Cooks

Patented!
Adjustable Steel Rods front and Back
"Balance the Load"

KUSTOM KNIVES™

Narrow HANDLES for
Small Fat Hands!
GERMAN MADE - ALL Styles

← Hand stiched
names

NORMAL WIDTH

← APRONS up to 55"
WAIST WITH PERSON-
ALIZED INSIGNIAS

10 GALLON

TOQUES

DOUBLE WIDE

Big'n Tall Chefs Attire
(1990)

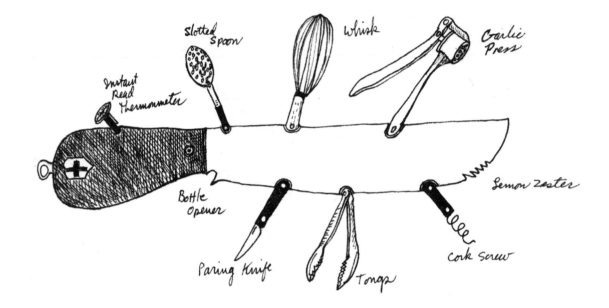

Swiss Chef's Knife
(1988)

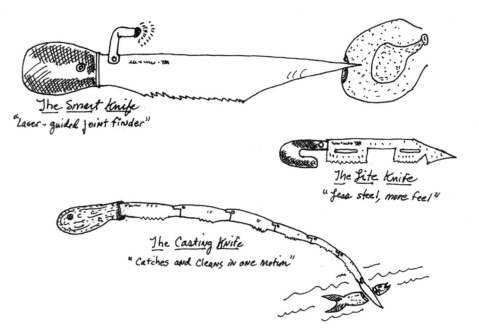

The Smart Knife
"Laser-guided joint finder"

The Lite Knife
"less steel, more feel"

The Casting Knife
"Catches and cleans in one motion"

On the Cutting Edge
(1991)

Restaurant Critic at Large

(1990)[†]

From the Jewish Chef: Bone Apetite!
(1990)[†]

Do you Chef Timothy wish to promote the Saucier Susan-Beth to be your Sous-Chef, to truss, confit and take stock together until your liaison separates?

When Chefs Marry

(1992)

Haute Cuisine Goes Haute Couture
(2008)

Executive or Head Chef
(Chef de Cuisine)

Under Chef
(Sous Chef)

Expediter
(Aboyeur)

Roast
(Rôtisseur)

Saute/Sauces
(Saucier)

Fish
(Poissonier)

Grill/BBQ
(Grillardin)

A Contemporary Kitchen Brigade
(2008)†

Pastry/Cakes
(Patissier)

Pantry/Salads
(Garde Manger)

Frying
(Fritturier)

PizzaMan
(Italian Stallion)

Hunter Gatherer
(Forager)

Dishwasher
(Chef de Plunge)

Janitorial/Recycler
(The Rat)

Chairman, Joint Chefs of Staff
(2008)

A Self-Serving Chef
(2008)

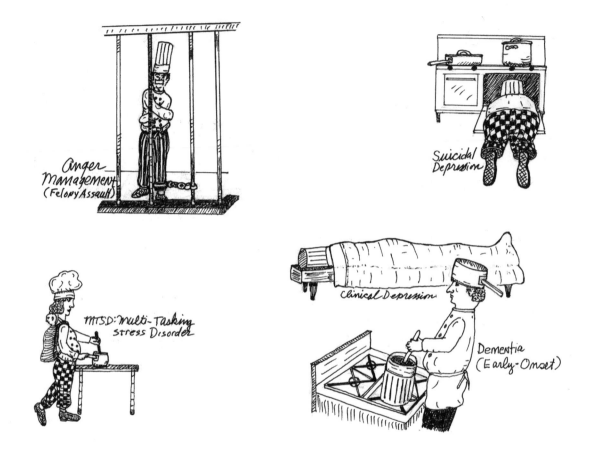

Typical Psychological Disorders in the Professional Kitchen
(2009)

Exhibitionism
(Compulsive Disorder)

Paranoia

Substance Abuse

Bipolar
(Martyr/Clown
complex)

Duck Hook          Pizza Slice          Veal Shank

When Chefs Play Golf
(2008)†

This new wave chef
made quite a splash

Surf 'n Turf

(2009)

Pumping Iron Chefs
(2008)

# Movements, Trends & Fashion

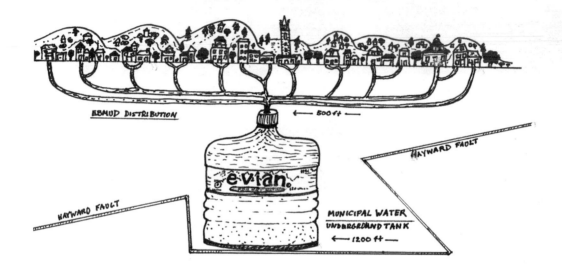

EBMUD DISTRIBUTION     ← 500 ft →

HAYWARD FAULT

HAYWARD FAULT

MUNICIPAL WATER
UNDERGROUND TANK
← 1200 ft →

From Berkeley's Office of Emergency Planning
(1990)

# THE BIRTH OF A GHETTO

uring the century of Berkeley history that preceded the designation of the Gourmet Ghetto as a California State Historic District (legal status pending application), mainstream Berkeley was, foodie-wise, just another small American town with a gastronomic IQ well below that of its brilliant but cranky population. Of course, small towns, especially those with big universities, can produce big personalities and unusual appetites. As the University of California at Berkeley blossomed in the 19th century, it became a powerful magnet for big personalities and unusual appetites in every field of human endeavor.* It was perhaps only a matter of time before the town known early on as the *Athens of the West* and more recently as *Berzerkeley* would discover, and then revolutionize, American gastronomy. Not surprisingly, therefore, it is documented that health food diets, vegetarianism and even raw foods regimens thrived among Berkeley's *fin de siecle* bohemian artists, poets, thespians, designers and intellectuals, as they would during the formative years of the Ghetto over a half century later.

CURATOR'S NOTE

*In this wing of MOCH we take a closer look at what has been labeled the revolution's "ground zero," Berkeley's fabled Gourmet Ghetto, before moving on to more general exhibits that reflect on various manifestations of the American food revolution. What took place gastronomically in the Ghetto in the 1970's is well-documented elsewhere at MOCH, as well as in a variety of books, documentaries, scholarly journals and food magazines. Yet to understand how the Ghetto came to contribute so much to an unprecedented merger of art, food, politics and lifestyle, one must examine more carefully its historical evolution.*

* Dave Weinstein's 2009 book, *It Came From Berkeley: How Berkeley Changed the World*, tells the story of Berkeley's out-sized influence on American and world culture.

There seems to be, in fact, an almost intrinsic connection between bohemian subcultures and adventurous eating, at least since the early 19th century. Mary Gluck in her book on Parisian bohemians, *Popular Bohemia* (2005), quotes from an 1831 article in Paris's *Le Figaro* on the qualities of the Parisian art crowd of the day, noting their "bizarre clothes, and their exotic tastes in food and interior decoration." Sounds like Berkeley's art/food crowd of the 1960's and 1970's.

One well-known proto foodie in Berkeley's early days — Bill "the Hot Dog Man" Henderson — is featured in Richard Schwartz's *Eccentrics, Heroes, and Cutthroats of Old Berkeley* (2007). Henderson, who operated food carts at various locations in Berkeley and Oakland, was celebrated as a hero in the early 1900's and was much loved for his antics as well as his extensive and witty hot dog menus. According to a 1919 article in the *Oakland Tribune*, "No man knows like William Henderson the low-down, ground-floor, rock-bottom secrets of the hot dog."

Narsai David with
Signature Bow Tie
(2009)

Curiously, as if the all-American hot dog has some deep resonance in Berkeley's cultural core, a half century after Henderson's reign as Mr. Hot Dog, Bruce Aidells, another big Berkeley personality, would revolutionize the old-fashioned commercial hot dog with his Aidells Sausage Company in the 1980's.

While local historians have given a feel for Old Berkeley and its larger-than-life characters, they only hint at what mainstream Berkeley was eating. The best evidence supports the idea that everyday eating in early Berkeley reflected the ethnic backgrounds of its residents. But by the 1950's and 1960's, cultural change was in the air and gourmet restaurateurs like the late Hank Rubin and his protégé and partner, Narsai David,* began to satisfy post-war hunger for adventurous continental cooking at restaurants like Cruchon's and Pot Luck, and then at David's popular Narsai's Restaurant in Kensington, on Berkeley's northern border. Still, if you wanted genuine haute cuisine, you went to San Francisco, the *Paris of the West*, where fancy French food arrived with the gold rush and its millionaires.

* Note Narsai's bow tie, the emblem of an old school connoisseur and bon vivant. His colorful private label neckwear line (floral bow ties and conventional neck ties) is available on the Narsai website (www.narsai.com) and at select Bay Area farmers' markets, along with Narsai's legendary Chocolate Decadence sauce and many other gourmet products he produces through Narsai's Specialty Foods, Inc. in Orinda, California. (Tell 'em MOCH sent you.)

Real gastronomic change (aka California cuisine) began in a small commercial enclave in the predominantly residential North Berkeley neighborhood near the corner of Shattuck Avenue and Vine Street. From the late 60's through the 70's this sleepy village, far from the student tumult of South Berkeley, would add one fancy-food establishment after another until eventually it would be heralded as the Gourmet Ghetto. First Peet's Coffee, then the Cheese Board, Chez Panisse, Pig-by-the-Tail Charcuterie, Cocolat, the Juice Bar Collective, Poulet and on and on it went into the 80's and 90's — Phoenix Pastificio, Saul's Deli, the Cheese Board's Pizza Collective, César, Masse's Pastries, Liaison Bistro and many others. To accommodate the Ghetto's growth, its borders were inching south toward downtown Berkeley.

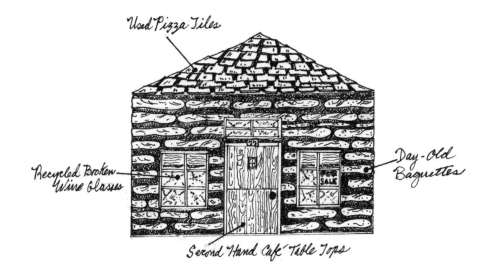

The Affordable New Recycled Berkeley Baguette House
(1990)

Ironically, what has been forgotten is that the term Gourmet Ghetto actually began as a joke, coined by comedian and Cheese Board Collective member Darryl Henriques.* A former member of the San Francisco Mime Troupe, Darryl introduced this oxymoronic expression in the mid-70's. He used it to amuse customers and fellow workers at the Cheese Board and then at venues like the Freight & Salvage Coffee House, where his stand-up comedy routines included mocking references to the new food-obsessed neighborhood.

The City of Berkeley defines "Gourmet Ghetto" today on its official website as a colloquial expression for Berkeley's infamous foodie neighborhood. Colloquial perhaps, but it becomes almost perverse when one considers the subliminal reference to Venice's 15th century *ghetta* ( meaning "slag," the byproduct of iron smelting), an area of foundries where Jews were forced to live in contaminated squalor. Nevertheless, at MOCH we accept the term Gourmet Ghetto as the de facto symbol of the historic neighborhood that changed the way America cooks and eats. Go figure!

* In fairness, it must be pointed out that there are competing claims for the term "Gourmet Ghetto." The late *San Francisco Chronicle* columnist Herb Caen has been credited with coining the term by a member of the North Shattuck Association, a Berkeley merchants' group. But Caen may have merely passed it along in a column from one of his informants in the East Bay. Longtime Berkeley resident, Cheese Board shopper and wry journalist Alice Kahn has also taken credit for the term, according to one Cheese Board member. Alice is the writer who first used the term "yuppie" in an early 1980's article in the *East Bay Express* which described Berkeley's growing community of young urban professionals. The yuppie phenomenon transformed the Ghetto, to be sure, and eventually other East Bay neighborhoods as well: The Elmwood, Rockridge, 4th Street and most recently, West Berkeley's Left Bank.

# HEROES OF THE GHETTO

ALFRED PEET
1920-2007
Peets Coffee
Tea & Spices

## ALFRED PEET ~ *The Original Mr. Coffee*

Peet's coffee had magic. How many thousands of customers have reported a Proustian reaction to their first cup of Mr. Peet's French roast? OK, only those that know Proust's novels, but then that's most of Berkeley. And Proust's narrator was drinking tea, not coffee, but that's beside the point. My first cup of Peet's was on a summer's day in 1968 and the psychic potency of that first cup flooded me with memories of my stay in Paris the previous summer. I returned to Peet's just about every day for the next fifteen or twenty years hoping to "re-Peet" that first transcendent cup.

I was so excited by the discovery of Peet's Coffee that I wanted to know the man behind the brew. Like a college professor who changes your life with an idea, Al Peet had changed mine with a cup of coffee. I tried to engage Mr. Peet behind his counter, but he was not the engaging type. No, Dutch-born Al Peet was quiet, taciturn and somewhat imperious in the Old World style, which many customers remember as simply crusty. He was a fine looking fellow, it should be noted, albeit with thinish lips and a prominent, not quite aquiline, nose — both well suited, it would appear, for cupping, the professional coffee-taster's practice.

Though Mr. Peet launched the Ghetto with his shop in 1966, he remained detached from the hubbub that exploded outside his store every morning — the crowd of poets, artists, hippies, politicos and other sundry types known as "Peetniks." Peet's operated, with or without Al Peet's blessing, as a traditional village shop where commerce and social networking are interconnected functions. But if Al Peet worked in the emerging Gourmet Ghetto he was never really *of* it. By the time the Ghetto was in full swing at the end of the 1970's, the spicy aromas of the Ghetto's professional kitchens perfuming the neighborhood's air as pungently as Peet's roasting beans, Peet had sold his growing company, staying on at Peet's Coffee behind the scenes as a coffee cupper, buyer and resident icon.

It is proudly claimed by veteran Peetniks, and the company's marketing department, that Al Peet's Old World approach to coffee — introducing arabica instead of the lesser quality robusta beans used by the commercial coffee industry — revolutionized Bay Area and indeed American coffee awareness. He turned American java into Mocha-Java and set the stage for our Starbucks Nation and the micro-roasting movement we see today. That said, however, word in the Ghetto persists that Mr. Peet, the man, privately if not secretly, preferred drinking tea, which I find amusing, if not hilarious.

At an event held at the Ghetto's flagship Peet's store on October 22, 2009 to dedicate the Alfred H. Peet Memorial Room (a small Peet's museum in the back of the store), I heard all kinds of comments about Peet from former employees, friends and colleagues that not only addressed questions regarding his beverage preferences, but much more: Was Peet a nice man, a tough boss, a congenial friend? Why did he never marry? Were his parents secret Jews who fooled the Dutch authorities during WWII? Did he really step on the feet of clerks behind the counter when he caught them giving inaccurate information to customers? The one piece of the Al Peet story that did get confirmed that night by one of his closest co-cuppers was his growing preference for tea over coffee as he got older.

Of course in the coffee-drinking universe beyond Berkeley and the Ghetto, where Peet's Coffee & Tea is the acknowledged pioneer of a new American coffee culture (not to be confused with Europe's café culture), no one really cares whether Al Peet was a nice guy or a curmudgeon, or even whether his beans were burnt and bitter, as some claim. And if Alfred Peet is forgotten today as a spice merchant, as the original name of the store would indicate he was (Peet's Coffee, Tea & Spices), or as a man who kept his tea preferences a trade secret, such is the editorial function of history, or as the British historian E. P. Thompson put it, the "enormous condescension of posterity."

At MOCH we honor both the legend of Al Peet, the Original Mr. Coffee, and the enigmatic and persnickety tea and spice lover behind the legend.

American To-Go Coffee Culture vs. European To-Stay Café Culture
(2010)

## SAHAG AVEDISIAN ~ *The Big Cheese*

One cannot imagine a more radical contrast with the Gourmet Ghetto's Original Mr. Coffee than the Ghetto's other godfather, the Big Cheese. Known as Sam and Sawdog to early *ghettoistas*, the Cheese Board's charismatic co-founder, Sahag Avedisian, was a rough, tough Armenian American from the poorer side of the tracks in Pawtucket, Rhode Island. Built like a prizefighter, with a naturally muscular upper body — he never liked that his legs were comparatively skinny — Sahag occasionally acted the part, even getting into one or two street fights that I can recall.

Though Sahag's mood swings, ranging from warm and generous to bitter and depressed, turned out to be a curse that ultimately broke him, day in and day out he was one of the funniest and most engaging men I'd ever met. A gifted physical comedian and ham, as well as a brilliant outside-the-box political and social thinker, Sahag was unique. From the moment the doors of the

SAHAG
AVEDISIAN
*1930-2007*
Cheese Board
Collective

Cheese Board opened in 1967 the community adored him. The way he threw his wit around, along with those huge wheels of cheddar cheese, there was no doubt that Sahag was the Ghetto's Big Cheese.

I don't think there was any love lost between Sahag and Al Peet, who had been, according to Ghetto lore, skeptical about the prospects for the new cheese store. After all, Dutch Peet was born with a silver coffee spoon in his mouth. Sahag, and his wife and shop partner, Meg, knew next to nothing about fine cheese, let alone fine food and wine, when they planned their mom and pop store. When Mr. Peet came into the Cheese Board after its first day of business, saw the impressive array of domestic and imported cheeses (about one hundred varieties compared to four hundred today) and heard that the store had grossed $95, he told the Avedisians, "You're going to make it!"

Inspired by his experiences on an Israeli kibbutz, Sahag took a bold step in 1971 when, together with Meg, he collectivized the Cheese Board, transferring ownership of the store for a song to its small group of employees. Perhaps emboldened by the explosive political and cultural climate of Berkeley and the Bay Area at the time, the Avedisians literally merged growing culinary awareness and radical politics into a worker-owned business, anticipating, it can be argued, some of the worker-rights components of the Italian-based Slow Food movement that would emerge almost two decades later. An unintended consequence of their socially progressive decision was that the Avedisians became, to their chagrin, heroes in the Ghetto and beyond. Sahag in particular was constantly sought after for business, political and personal advice, which, depending on his mood, he liked to share.

I received some of Sahag's patented advice while promoting *The Book of Garlic* in 1977. When I defended garlic breath in a mock debate on TV in New York with a chemist representing Lever Brothers' new mouthwash product, Signal, their PR department was so pleased with the audience response that they offered to fly me around the country for a national debate on mouthwash vs. garlic breath. When I got back to Berkeley, I conferred with Sahag who agreed that it would be very good for book sales to accept the Signal offer. But, Sahag pointed out, this was a textbook example of how corporate interests co-opt revolutions. His suggestion was to do the tour but keep the debate "real" by offering to pay my own travel expenses. I agreed, sent my counter-offer off in the mail, and never heard from Signal's PR team again. So much for the garlic book's elevation to the national "best-smeller" lists!

This was, in fact, pretty standard advice from Sahag: "Don't sell out!" And Sahag, to his credit, lived his own principles, though he increasingly used those principles to rain on the Cheese Board's parade. He hated the fact that the Board was attracting increasing media attention, sometimes in the wake of Chez Panisse's rising star across the street, fearing that it would ultimately corrupt the store.

When former Cheese Board employee Bob Klein produced a short documentary on the Board for KPIX Channel 5 in 1976, Sahag reluctantly agreed to be interviewed. It was clear from his abrupt and surly answers to Bob's on-camera questions that Sahag was not happy about the flattering documentary, merely using it for his own purposes — to make it clear to a large Bay Area audience that as good as it was, the Cheese Board's collectivist structure yielded less than a perfect workers' paradise.

By the late 80's, with his dark side in full bloom, Sahag resigned from the Cheese Board Collective. After a brief stint working at the Juice Bar Collective on Vine St., which he had helped to open in 1975, he took off for good in 1992 to roam the country in his Ford Escort station wagon. From the road Sahag would send to some of us his sometimes brilliant but almost illegible hand-written political manifestos mixed with mea culpas and his old standby mottos, like "If the world doesn't become a summer camp, it'll become a concentration camp." Occasionally he would show up unannounced in Berkeley for brief visits. But his final years where spent alone and more or less in silence, holed up in an Ann Arbor, Michigan, hotel.

At MOCH we celebrate the Big Cheese for his progressive contributions to the Ghetto and greater Berkeley.

WAVY GRAVY
1936-
Social Activist
Clown

**WAVY GRAVY ~** *Ice Cream Flavor*

I include in my personal Ghetto pantheon Berkeley's notorious activist clown and ageless hippy, Wavy Gravy, aka Hugh Romney. Never a resident or worker in the Ghetto, and not identified with gastronomy (though his Hog Farm kitchen at Woodstock did serve granola), Wavy is nevertheless celebrated at MOCH not only for his gastro-comic surname and antic counter-cultural persona, but for his eponymous Ben & Jerry's ice cream flavor, "Wavy Gravy."* This really got my attention, and I can't help but speculate that had I stuck with my Mr. Garlic persona in the 1970's with the same commitment to garlic justice as Mr. Gravy had to social justice, I might have ended up with my own ice cream flavor too — "Mr. Garlic." Caramelized garlic, date puree and chocolate chips swirled into a rich vanilla/honey custard.

* Gravy has told MOCH that his flavor was cancelled after Ben & Jerry's was bought out by the Unilever company. There is a grass roots effort to reinstate the flavor.

## BRUCE AIDELLS ~ *The Sausage King*

Athough his fame as the Sausage King came from work outside the Ghetto, Bruce launched his eponymous sausage company following a stint in the Ghetto as the first chef at Marilyn Rinzler's homage to chicken, Poulet, which opened in 1979. I had known Bruce in high school and gastronomic trivia lovers will delight in knowing that "Big Bruce" was a varsity cheerleader at University High School in West Los Angeles in 1962, the same year I was on the track team throwing the shot put.

Then, when Dr. Bruce Aidells, a Ph.D. biologist at the University of California, was transitioning from cancer research to professional cooking, he met Marilyn, Berkeley's Chicken Lady, who was planning her Frenchie deli and chicken-to-go shop. On a day that vividly stands out in my memory, I brought Bruce along with a group of Berkeley foodist friends, including Marilyn, headed to a fund-raising event in Marin County where Julia Child was appearing. This was the day we all met Julia for the first time — we stood in a long reception line waiting, in awe, to shake her hand. I recall noting that she was old enough to be my mother and tall enough to be my father.

BRUCE AIDELLS[†]
1944-
CHEF
AUTHOR

This was also the day that Marilyn and Bruce met and clicked, or should I say clucked? After appropriate due diligence, including a meal Bruce cooked for us at Marilyn's house, which featured the sausages he had been making for Le Picnique on College Ave., Bruce was hired by Marilyn and now had a toehold at the edge of the expanding Ghetto, on the corner of Shattuck Ave. and Virginia St.

It was at Bruce's house in the Kensington hills that same year, 1979, that Les Blank shot a scene for his film, *Garlic Is As Good As Ten Mothers*, featuring Bruce and the extraordinary Anzonini del Puerto, an Andalusian flamenco singer, dancer and sausage maker living at the time with Cheese Boarder Pat Darrow. I had urged Anzonini to come up with a song about garlic for Les's film and he performed it, accompanied by guitarist Kenny Parker, while Bruce made Anzonini's chorizo recipe in the kitchen. Having sold his wildly successful Aidells Sausage Company in 2002, Bruce Aidells currently writes cookbooks about meat, launches product lines, hosts TV shows and eats well at Boulevard Restaurant in San Francisco where his wife, Nancy Oakes, is co-owner and chef.

## BOB WAKS ~ *The Communard*

Wax Angel
(1970)[†]

Bob is one of the most colorful and notorious of the Ghetto's under-sung heroes. His capacity for merging brilliant cooking, talented singing and around-the-clock partying is legendary, if not controversial. Even today Bob will belt out falsetto tunes after barbequing deeply flavored ribs, chicken wings and pork butts at *al fresco* catering gigs. He will whip out his country fiddle, too, if a group starts up.

I met Bob in Michael Haimovitz's summer art class at Cal in 1968, that same summer I discovered Peet's and the Cheese Board. By the fall, Bob and I were both working at the Cheese Board and living in Michael's art commune on Colby St. in Oakland. Bob became, by default, the commune's designated cook — no one in the group loved to cook as much as Bob, nor did it as well. The French have a word for the chef who cooks for a restaurant's staff — the *communard*. That's Bob, wherever he has lived or worked.

For the record, Michael's "art form" was a bit of a scandal in the U.C. Berkeley Art Department at the time. His intricately staged "events," which Bob and I began working on as soon as we had moved into Colby St., took a targeted individual on a series of disorienting environmental escapades which often included an "unusual" meal. At one such event for a professor at Cal who lectured on surrealism, he was served an elegant dinner made up of ultra-tiny food portions — baby quail's legs, under-developed English peas, thumb-sized dinner rolls, slices of a tiny chocolate cake — all presented on children's plates with child-sized silver and glassware. Those at the table that night later reported feeling uncomfortably large or oddly distanced from the food — in a word, surreal!

Bob and I had found our Berkeley niche! We were Cheese Board clerks by day and by night surrealist artist/cooks on Michael Haimovitz's magical mystery tour.

In the summer of 1971, Bob and I took another fateful step together. Alice Waters had come to the Cheese Board to ask for help in opening Chez Panisse and we answered her siren call. While I didn't last very long as a waiter, Bob stayed on in various official and unofficial capacities. He is still remembered fondly by the cooks of that era for the phenomenal staff meals he would put together after closing, using leftover components of dishes served that day. He is also remembered for the night in 1975 when he launched a naked "streak"* with Sahag Avedisian and others through the restaurant after a dinner celebrating a Cheese Boarder's birthday. I was at the meal but I didn't join the streak. I had no problem with being naked in public or streaking per se. In fact, I had recently played poker *à la nude* with Bob Waks and Bob Klein on a small stage at an art gallery in Berkeley's Live Oak Park. We described our little poker shtick as an "event," the term "performance art" not yet in common usage, at least in Berkeley. "Happenings" we associated with New York's art scene.

Although Bob continued to moonlight at Chez Panisse throughout the 1970's, his primary focus was still the Cheese Board. His role at the Board, as it was at Chez Panisse and Colby St., was, again, that of the *communard*. Not that the Board approved of Bob's self-appointed position as the collective's cook. In fact, it was an on-going complaint by several Cheese Boarders, especially Sahag, who could be quite tough on Bob, that he was cooking all day, not "working."

But the consequences of Bob's "artistic" work habits were nevertheless profound when he began to fool around with sourdough bread baking. With contributions by Cheese Boarder Eric Sartenaer and others, Bob's soon-to-be-celebrated Cheese Board baguettes were born by the late-70's, as a bread revolution rippled through the Bay Area and beyond. World-class bakeries followed the Cheese Board's lead, including Sartenaer's Semifreddi's bakery (sold in 1984 to its current owner) and former Chez Panisse busboy Steve Sullivan's Acme Bread Company.

MOCH celebrates the Ghetto's *communard* and his important contributions to the Bay Area's artisanal bread-baking traditions.

---

* I think Bob's impulse to streak through Chez Panisse was more a sophomoric prank than it was an "anarcho-syndicalist protest" against the restaurant's growing elitism, as has been asserted in one published history of Chez Panisse. Streaking as a social phenomenon blossomed, after all, at fraternities on college campuses in the 1960's.

**Tea Cup Lady**
(2003)†

## HELEN GUSTAFSON ~ *The Tea Lady*

The late Helen Gustafson was Berkeley's beloved Tea Lady — she launched the Chez Panisse tea program in the 1980's and wrote several books on the subject, including *The Agony of the Leaves* (1996). I had worked with Helen at The Swallow café in U.C. Berkeley's Art Museum in the 1970's, and after becoming neighbors in 2000 we were frequent afternoon tea partners in the English style, often joined by her husband Gus, and friends. Helen's vivacious personality, and her long association with Chez Panisse, made her a popular character in the Ghetto. In a culture where a cup of tea meant a tea bag and lukewarm water, Helen put up a noble struggle to raise tea standards, picking up with tea, in a sense, where Alfred Peet's coffee revolution left off. It was Helen who first alerted me, in a conspiratorial whisper, that Al Peet preferred drinking tea to coffee!

I joined Helen's tea crusade after developing an aversion to the taste of my morning cup of drip coffee — after two decades of Peet's virile brew, I was ready for something new. I began exploring tea as an alternative. Although Helen became my "tea-cher," and her sharing of extraordinary and rare teas was always appreciated, I confess that the pots of tea she served me at her house tasted, well, weak. On the other hand, my style of serving black tea was, according to Helen, "over-brewed." She was correct, technically speaking, but I was looking for strong flavor and a caffeinated punch to replace coffee, not the delicate and nuanced beverage she promoted at Chez Panisse and in her books. Nevertheless, Helen and I worked it out, alternating our afternoons between subtle tea at her house and strong tea at mine.

My cherished collection of vintage tea cups is made up largely of hand-me-downs, some purchased, some gifted, from Helen's wonderful collection, each one a vivid and charming reminder of her. The Tea Lady is much missed in the Ghetto and at tea time chez moi.

## ALICE WATERS ~ *The Ghetto's Queen Bee*

Much has been written about the final exhibit in my pantheon of Ghetto heroes and the factors — biographical, political, cultural and counter-cultural — that have shaped the Ghetto's Queen Bee. The early years of Alice's collaboration with Jeremiah Tower, and the endorsements by the East Coast's culinary elite — especially James Beard — had put Chez Panisse at the forefront of an exciting gastronomic movement. It came to be known by the 1980's as California cuisine, but it had a broad national impact and has in recent years comingled with influences from abroad, including Italy's Slow Food movement.

By the 1990's, Alice's restaurant increasingly functioned as her busy beehive, sending out its storied message into the greater culinary world on the wings of its talented chef/pollinators. Once free of the hive's gravitational pull, these anointed *cuisiniers* have often blossomed in their own right, creating restaurant, cookbook and even product-line empires of their own — Victoria Wise, Mark Miller, Judy Rodgers, Jonathan Waxman, Joyce Goldstein, Christopher Lee and Paul Bertolli are notable examples.

Although we have attempted to establish the contemporary culinary context of Chez Panisse's breakthroughs in the 1970's, MOCH's curatorial explorations go back to an even earlier period of progressive cultural, social and aesthetic aspiration in England and Europe — the Arts and Crafts movement of the late 19th and early 20th centuries — to explain the evolving food aesthetic, not merely the Craftsman décor,* of Chez Panisse.

| JOHN RUSKIN | WILLIAM MORRIS | BERNARD MAYBECK | JULIA MORGAN | ALICE WATERS |
|---|---|---|---|---|
| *1819–1900* | *1834–1896* | *1862–1957* | *1872–1957* | *1944–* |
| Art Critic & Social Thinker | Arts & Crafts Designer & Social Reformer | Visionary Arts & Crafts Architect | Pioneering Woman Architect | Restaurateur & Culinary Arts Reformer |

### On the Road to Arts & Crafts Cooking

(2009)

* Architect-trained Jeremiah Tower did notice the physical Arts and Crafts details at Chez Panisse as described in his memoir, *California Dish*: "The remodeled old Victorian house looked like a cross between Frank Lloyd Wright and Charles Rennie Mackintosh, with a little bow to Berkeley's Julia Morgan."

MOCH presents the story of Alice Waters, the architect of what she has dubbed a "Delicious Revolution," in terms of a pre-existing aesthetic condition in Berkeley and the Bay Area. It has been argued that Northern California, and especially the East Bay communities of Piedmont and Berkeley, was the epicenter of California's historic identification with the Arts and Crafts aesthetic and progressive social ideals of England's William Morris and his mentor, John Ruskin. (See Leslie Freudenheim's 2005 book, *Building with Nature*.) Layered over the aesthetics was the vision of California as an anti-materialist, anti-industrial and socially progressive Garden of Eden. The historian Kevin Starr writes about California along these same lines as a California "dream."

Connecting Alice Waters and Chez Panisse to the foundations of Berkeley's early Zeitgeist is best conveyed by comparing Ms. Water's book, *The Art of Simple Food* (2007), to Charles Keeler's 1904 classic, *The Simple Home*, a book that proselytized Arts and Crafts design and architectural concepts, many attributable to Morris and to Keeler's close friend and mentor, the architect Bernard Maybeck. One of Keeler's opening lines in the book could have been uttered at the dawn of the California cuisine movement — just place the word "culinary" in front of Keeler's "art":

> *A movement toward a simpler, a truer, a more vital [culinary] art expression is now taking place in California.*

Keeler, a popular local poet, playwright, naturalist and founder of The Cosmic Religion, was a force in Berkeley's bohemian and civic sets which included painter William Keith, naturalist John Muir and developer Duncan McDuffie. In *The Simple Home* he advocated principles that resonate uncannily with those in *The Art of Simple Food*.

The comparisons are stark. Here's a partial list:

| SIMPLE HOME (KEELER) | SIMPLE FOOD (WATERS) |
| --- | --- |
| • highest quality materials | • highest quality ingredients |
| • locally sourced materials | • locally sourced ingredients |
| • structural elements left exposed | • food that tastes like what it is |
| • hand-made interior accessories | • cooking by hand/no gadgets |
| • flower gardens for the soul | • kitchen gardens for the meal |
| • hearths for family connection | • hearths for family cooking |

Opening Night Service
at Chez Panisse
(1981)[†]

Is it now possible to conclude that Berkeley's earliest aesthetic and social reform aspirations have resurfaced through the Ruskinian polemics of a Delicious Revolution? Has the 19th century Arts and Crafts movement been resurrected through Alice Waters to lend support to a late 20th-century gastronomic awakening in America? Perhaps this narrative is best left for future scholars to evaluate. Meanwhile, MOCH will continue to celebrate the Ghetto's Queen Bee with exhibits that explore the growing legend and its relationship to Berkeley's unique cultural inheritance.

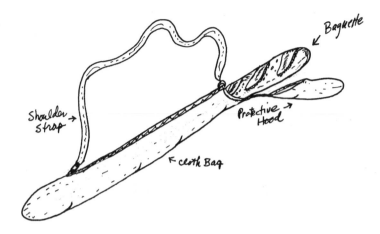

Baguette

Shoulder Strap →

Protective Hood →

← cloth Bag

← Shopper

Berkeley Baguette Bag
(1988)[†]

Farm-Raised Bass at Harvest Time
(1992)[†]

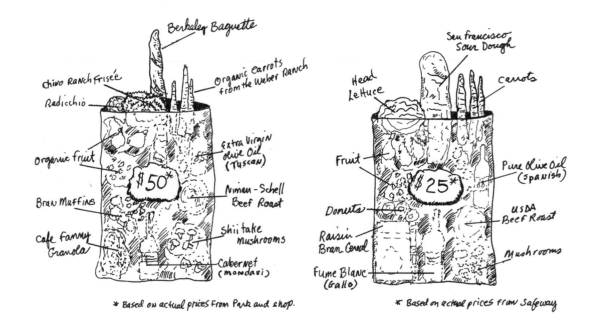

Berkeley Baguette

Chino Ranch Frisée

Radicchio

Organic carrots from the Weber Ranch

Organic Fruit

Extra Virgin Olive Oil (Tuscan)

$50*

Bran Muffins

Niman - Schell Beef Roast

Cafe Fanny Granola

Shiitake mushrooms

Cabernet (Mondavi)

* Based on actual prices from Park and shop.

San Francisco Sour Dough

Head Lettuce

Carrots

Fruit

Pure Olive Oil (Spanish)

$25*

Donuts

USDA Beef Roast

Raisin Bran Cereal

Fume Blanc (Gallo)

Mushrooms

* Based on actual prices from Safeway

The New American Cooking = the Old American Cooking x 2
(1990)[†]

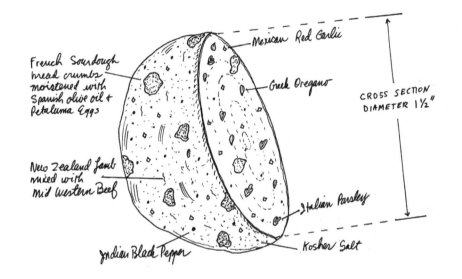

French Sourdough bread crumbs moistened with Spanish olive oil & Petaluma Eggs

Mexican Red Garlic

Greek Oregano

CROSS SECTION DIAMETER 1½"

New Zealand Lamb mixed with mid western Beef

Italian Parsley

Indian Black Pepper

Kosher Salt

Multinational "Greek" Meatball (Keftedes universalis)
(1990)†

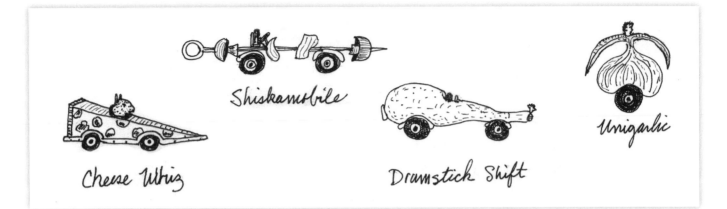

Cheese Whiz

Shiskamobile

Drumstick Shift

Unigarlic

Street Food

(1990)†

The New French "S Car Go"

(2008)

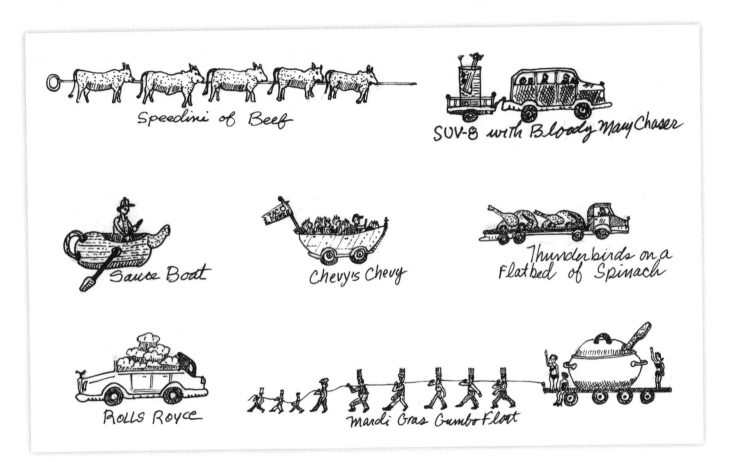

More Meals on Wheels

(2008)

Truffle Hunting in Piedmont
(2008)[†]

At the Olive Harvest, Two Extra Virgins Look On
(2009)†

From Farm to Table: Getting to Know Your Local Ingredients
(2009)

Porkey's Revenge
(2007)[†]

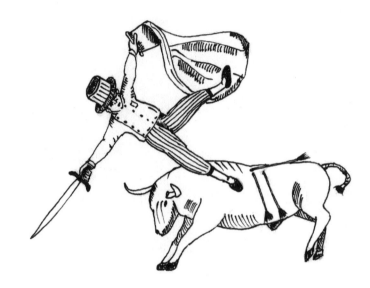

Grass Fed Up Beef
(2008)[†]

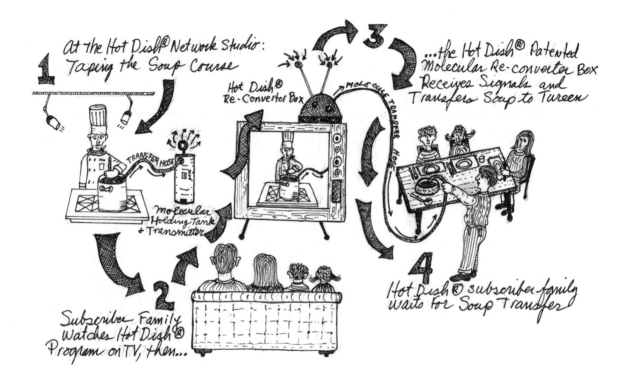

**1** At the Hot Dish® Network Studio: Taping the Soup Course

TRANSFER HOSE

Molecular Holding Tank + Transmitter

Hot Dish® Re-Converter Box

MOLECULE TRANSFER HOSE

**3** ...the Hot Dish® Patented Molecular Re-converter Box Receives Signals and Transfers Soup to Tureen

**2** Subscriber Family Watches Hot Dish® Program on TV, then...

**4** Hot Dish® subscriber family waits for Soup Transfer

When the TV Dinner Meets Molecular Gastronomy
(2009)

At the Farmers Market
(2008)[†]

# Miscellaneous Eating Disorders

If Dracula Ate Steak
(1987)

# THE FORGOTTEN STOMACH

*A* hundred years ago, a skinny chef might have rued his fate. His lack of rotundity reflected poorly on his professional status within the trade. Hence the old adage, "Never trust a skinny chef." I would not have had his problem. Growing up in the 1950's in a family where women were trim and swanky, and the men big and beefy, I've vacillated all my life, morphologically speaking, between husky and plump. Neither describes the more ectomorphic body type that I, and the women in my life, have wished for me.

But when exactly did thin come in? As I understand it, roughly at the end of the 19th century, when prodigious male girth as a sign of wealth and status began to shrink under doctor's orders. M.F.K. Fisher acknowledged the shift in her entry on Gluttony in *An Alphabet for Gourmets* (1949):

> *Probably this country will never again see so many fat, rich men as were prevalent at the end of the last century, copper kings and railroad millionaires and suchlike literally stuffing themselves to death in imitation of Diamond Jim, whose abnormally large stomach coincided so miraculously with the period.*

At the same time, women were told by their doctors that if they wanted to shrink their tummies, hips and bottoms, they would have to give up their prized symbol of feminine beauty, a voluptuous décolleté.

Gourmets and gourmands of both genders were suddenly faced with heretofore undiagnosed conditions classified as eating disorders and addiction. Diet (the kind of food you eat) became dieting (the kind of food you can't eat). The notoriously obese journalist and gourmet A. J. Liebling reflected on this new orientation to hunger and body type in his *Between Meals*, quoting the proprietor of one of his favorite Paris restaurants in the 1930's:

> *Only twenty-five percent of my customers order a plat du jour... The rest take grilled things. It's the doctors, you know. People think only of the liver and the figure. The stomach is forgotten.*

Another late great gourmet of Liebling's generation was Ludwig Bemelmans, a culinary memoirist and artist most famous for his Madeline children's books which he wrote and illustrated in the 1940's and 50's. I don't know what Bemelmans' waistline measured in his maturity, but he handled the growing cultural pressure against over-indulgent gourmandizing with literary aplomb:

> *Psychologists say that an excessive intake of food and wine is a substitute for happiness. I like pudding, I like wine, roast goose, Virginia ham, shepherd's pie, and lobster stew.*

This is taken from Mr. Bemelmans' 1955 novel, *To the One I Love the Best*, which celebrated his dear friend, the famous interior decorator, Elsie de Wolfe (Lady Mendl), then living in Hollywood where Bemelmans had come to write anti-Nazi screenplays in the 1940's.

I had not yet read Mr. Bemelmans' novel when I was first confronted with my own eating disorder. It was while in Spain in the summer of 1991 that the new lady in my life diagnosed a vague yet pervasive condition that has, apparently, haunted me since childhood. I was hoping that a romantic trip with a new love to one of Europe's gastronomic capitals might spark the next phase in my career, or a second marriage — not a mental health intervention!

On our way from Madrid to Barcelona, as I began to lay out my ambitious plans for eating in Catalonia, my travel companion offered her professional opinion: "Your entire career in food, even your precious *Book of Garlic*, are just manifestations of your addiction to food." She went further: "You've cleverly constructed your life to facilitate and at the same time hide an obsession with eating." An addiction *and* an obsession! I was outraged and responded defensively. "Sure," I told her, "I eat a lot, and often, and think a lot about food, and often. And yes," I continued, "I have written about food and published others who have written about food. My life *is* food! OK. But is that a disease?"

Years later I came to understand that the line between one's happy passions and destructive behaviors is, well, thin. What could I really say, though, to my over-educated diagnostician? She had a double master's degree in nutrition and psychology and had worked with eating-disorder patients in clinics and private practice. But did I have to deal with it right there, in a car speeding toward the gastronomic heart of Catalan cooking and my first real taste of some of the world's best food?*

Obsessive      Compulsive
(1990/2008)

So there I was in Barcelona, bound up in a culinary straightjacket, forced to visit all its art and architectural marvels. Swallowing my pride, I limited my culinary explorations to Barcelona's popular restaurants, many serving only mediocre tourist dishes. Then, once back home, I put my condition out of my mind and the woman out of my life. I didn't think again about her, or my alleged disorder, until I came across Bemelmans' novel many years later in the library of a friend's apartment in Paris.

---

* I had eaten Catalan dishes at recipe testing sessions for Marimar Torres' 1992 cookbook, *Catalan Country Cooking*, but that was at her home in Sausalito, California, not Barcelona, Spain.

I had read some of his Madeline books with my children, but I had never encountered any of Bemelmans' humorous illustrated memoirs about his years in the hotel and restaurant trade, or his fiction. In his narrative about Ms. de Wolfe, Bemelmans considers the inevitability of death in relation to the pleasures of the table:

> I am hungry and thirsty a great deal of the time, which accounts for the fact that I have acquired a reputation as a connoisseur of wines and as a gourmet. If I am hungry, then, the thing I worry about most is that one day all the goodies will be taken away from me.

For Bemelmans, death was a permanent end to gourmandizing, the loss of "all the goodies." Literally true, I thought, poignant and yet rather neurotic when put in that way. But could one attribute his classic literary/culinary stories compiled in books like *Hotel Splendide* (1941) and *Hotel Bemelmans* (1946), which I devoured on returning home from Paris, solely to a "condition?" Doesn't one need a prodigious talent, along with a disorder, to produce works of such quality and appeal?

If I could take that trip to Spain over again and muster the gastro-testicular fortitude (*cojones*) of the great Ludwig Bemelmans, I would embrace my condition, and my Diamond Jim belly, and respond "Yes, of course!" before dumping my borderline anorexic companion at the Barcelona airport for a flight home. What a lost opportunity! To think that I could have stayed on alone in Catalonia, me and my always hungry stomach, gorging on the region's glorious goodies. To paraphrase my literary/culinary hero: I like *pa amb tomaquet*, I like *paella*, I like anything with *romesco* sauce and *allioli*, and I'd die happy in a giant vat of *crema catalana*.

Home Cooking
(2008)

A la Cart Dinner for Six
(1988)

Pot Luck
(2005)

Shrimp on the Grill
(1989)

Boeuffet
(1985)

118

Shark Skin Suit

Stuffed Potato Couch

Saddle of Lamb

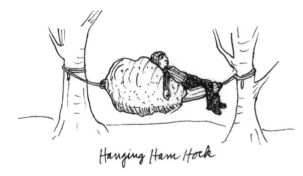

Hanging Ham Hock

Bed of Lettuce

Comfort Food

(2009)

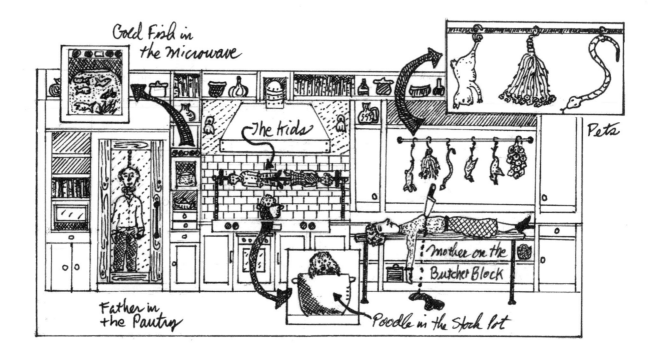

Family Meals with Pet Food Details

(2008)

His Dream Kitchen
(2008)[†]

The Eight Hundred Pound Turkey in the Room
(2008)

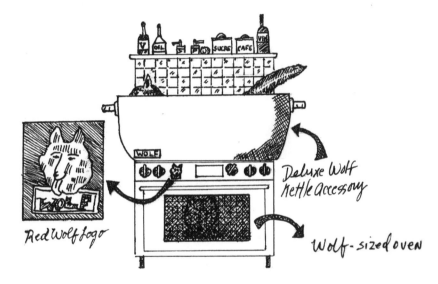

Red Wolf Logo

Deluxe Wolf Kettle Accessory

Wolf-sized oven

How to Cook a Wolf on a Wolf
(2008)<sup>†</sup>

High Tea
(2008)[†]

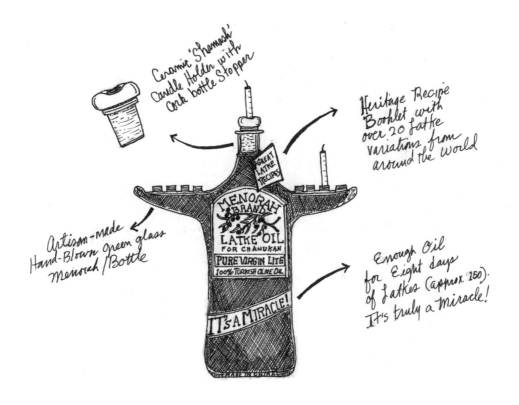

Ceramic 'Shamash' Candle Holder with Cork bottle Stopper

Heritage Recipe Booklet with over 20 Latke variations from around the world

GREAT LATKE RECIPES

MENORAH BRAND LATKE OIL FOR CHANUKAH
PURE VIRGIN LITE
100% TURKISH OLIVE OIL

IT's A MIRACLE!

Artisan-made Hand-Blown green glass Menorah / Bottle

Enough Oil for Eight days of Latkes (approx. 150). It's truly a Miracle!

Chanukah Miracle Menorah

(2009)

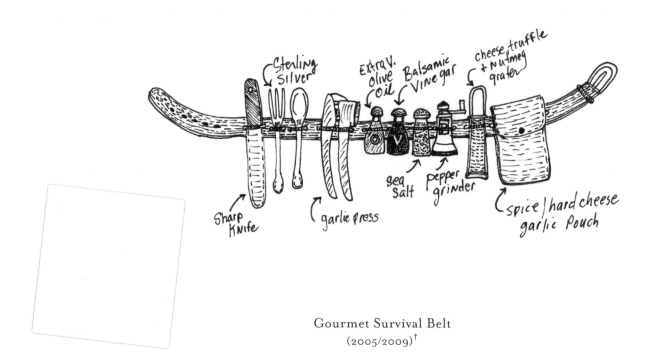

Sterling
Silver

Extra V.
olive
oil

Balsamic
Vinegar

cheese, truffle
+ Nutmeg
grater

Sharp
Knife

garlic press

Sea
Salt

Pepper
grinder

spice/hard cheese
garlic Pouch

Gourmet Survival Belt
(2005/2009)[†]

# *Les Desserts*

AN ANECDOTAL, CHRONOLOGICAL
CATALOG OF FOODOODLES

BIBLIOGRAPHY

ACKNOWLEDGEMENTS

ABOUT THE AUTHOR

*It is far from the purpose or desire of the author to add another to the innumerable volumes having practical cookery as their theme — the published works of the past decade alone being too numerous to digest.*

— George H. Ellwanger, *The Pleasures of the Table*, 1902

# An Anecdotal, Chronological Catalog of Foodoodles

## 1970—1992

1970   Hero on a Flying T-bone          *page 22*

†1970  Wax Angel          *page 92*

Next door to the Cheese Board's original location on Vine St. was a toy store, the Tree House. The owners were struggling to stay open in 1970 and I offered to produce a children's play that would be performed in the store to increase their business. The idea for a kid's *Commedia del Arte* production came out of skits I improvised at the Renaissance Pleasure Faire in Marin's Black Point forest where Bob Waks and I operated a Cheese Board concession in 1969. The doodle of Wax Angel represents one of the clown characters intended for the Tree House production. I had the theater bug at the time, and was taking dance and movement classes, one of them with Berkeley's very own Paris-trained mime and teacher, Leonard Pitt. Sadly, the Tree House had to close its doors before I could finish the script.

†1981  Opening Night Service at Chez Panisse          *page 97*
> *For Alice Waters and Chez Panisse*

This self-portrait as a waiter was drawn on the 10th anniversary of the opening of Chez Panisse. When a definitive history of the California cuisine movement is finally written, the night of August 28, 1971, will be

### Curator's Note

*All of the Foodoodles exhibited in the Museum of Culinary History are listed below in two chronological sections: 1970-1992 and 2003-2010. Within any particular year, the cartoons are listed in the order in which they appear in the book. Where an exhibit is identified with two dates (e.g., 2005/2009), the Foodoodle was started on the earlier date and completed on the later. Archived in this section of the museum are a series of short texts that function as backstory for many of the Foodoodles — dedications, sources, anecdotes, homages, etc.*

highlighted as arguably the transformative moment when an American food revolution first made itself known. Aging Berkeley foodists are already asking each other where they were that night and, according to veteran Chez Panisse host, Steve Crumley, "Literally thousands have claimed to have been there." And while not of equal historical magnitude as, say, the question "Where were you the day Kennedy was shot?", in terms of American food culture we are talking equivalent gravitas. Though no one was aware of it at the time, shots were fired on opening night at Chez Panisse and I was, willy-nilly, on the firing line. Looking at the drawing today, it's obvious that I forgot that the table cloths that night were red and white checked, and I'm surprised to see that I was wearing a tie. I don't believe

I was instructed to wear one but must have taken the evening very seriously. I've got the plate of duck right. The dish was created by Victoria Kroyer, who's better known today as Victoria Wise. She remembers, of course, the painstaking preparation of the classic French braise served that night. The name of the dish, as she recalls it, was *Duck aux Olives*, which varies from the name offered in previous histories — *Canard aux olives*. For Victoria, the distinction is very important. With its bilingual blend of French and English, "Duck aux Olives" symbolized for Victoria…

*… the state of grace with which we started Chez Panisse, giving ourselves permission to fly as we would to make good food, good fun and good politics.* *

This "state of grace" was fulfilled over the next decade as French classics were deconstructed and reconstructed by Chez Panisse chefs until the restaurant's trademark approach to fine cooking and dining emerged and proliferated.

I remember that night the lines of customers at the front door and the chaos in the kitchen. The servers were bumping into each other going through the swinging door from the dining room. I enjoyed bumping into Bebe, the French girl who was later reported to have been wearing a short shirt with no underwear. I can't personally verify that claim.

The one memory that is most vivid and poignant for me is serving Sahag Avedisian. After his dinner he handed me a $5 tip, which was more than the $3.95 price of the prix fixe meal and a symbolic gesture in a night filled with them. The arrival of Chez Panisse was a big deal for the neighborhood, though we had no clue how big, and the significance of Sahag's presence on that first night was understood by all, a blessing from the Big Cheese. I tore the $5 bill in two and gave one of the halves back to Sahag. We hugged goodbye and vowed someday we'd tape the bill back together and use it for a meal together at Chez Panisse. I don't remember if we did.

* From a personal communication.

I don't recall the impulse to illustrate Ms. David's "Rillettes de Lapin/Potted Rabbit and Pork" from my copy of her classic 1960 *French Provincial Cooking*. It might have been just the pun of "potted" animals simmering together in David's Provencal stock pot that attracted me. Then, when I began writing about the collaboration between Alice Waters and Jeremiah Tower at Chez Panisse and their shared love of Elizabeth David's culinary aesthetic, the illustration morphed into a caricature, if not a Foodoodle per se. Which animal represents which of my heroes is left to the reader's imagination. My copy of the Elizabeth David cookbook belonged first to my mother, a gift to her from my brother, Steve, and me, to thank her for sending us on a summer tour of Europe in 1963. My brother was attending the Sorbonne for his college's junior year abroad program and I went to meet him in Paris and begin our Grand Tour together. I was 15 and he 19.

That trip opened my eyes and taste buds. Like most of my generation of foodists, I can report a culinary epiphany in France. I don't think there have been so many culinary epiphanies since the first generation of humans who tasted meat cooked over an open fire. Mine was a sublime dish I had at the home where Steve was staying while attending the Sorbonne. Madame Pelletier's unbelievably rich Quiche Lorraine was the most exquisite thing I had ever tasted—the cream, the cheese, the eggs, the bacon! The "mouth feel" of that dish lingers, and has never been equaled by any quiche since. Taste memory is hard to match, especially when touched by the sublime.

There are two inscriptions to my mother in my copy of *French Provincial Cooking*, which came back to me after she passed away. One is my brother's in French, showing off his Sorbonne-acquired fluency. The other is mine, written in English: "To Mom, I hope this book adds to your already flourishing knowledge of the art of fine cuisine."

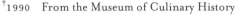

I used this image for the front of a seasonal greeting card sent out by Aris Books and Addison-Wesley Publishing Co. in 1990, after the sale of Aris to AW.

The baguette bag concept was partly inspired by the "Save-A-Tree" canvas shopping bags that Kim Marienthal, today a successful Berkeley real estate agent, created in 1971 and sold through the Co-op Market on Shattuck, which is now Andronico's. Of course I have never produced (or intended to produce) my baguette bag, or any of the products that have been invented as Foodoodles. One day in the mid-2000's, I walked into the Cheese Board and there it was, the "Baguette Quiver." This bread sack is made of bamboo cloth from China and was created by Ann Arnold, an artist and long-time Ghetto shopper.

The idea of using garlic clinically as an immersion therapy came to my attention while researching *The Book of Garlic*. I discovered a book, *Garlic, The Unknown Miracle Worker*, by Yoshio Kato, which tells the story of the garlic

therapy system known as "Flow-Leben" (flow of life) offered at the Oyama Garlic Laboratory in Amagasaki, Japan. The therapy is delivered by a machine with many small shower nozzles that spray patients with a garlic solution in various concentrations and targeted to areas of the body depending on the ailment being treated. I sold many copies of the Flow-Leben book through the *Garlic Times* newsletter which went to all members of Lovers of the Stinking Rose from the mid-1970's into the early 80's.

As I look back on this first "museum" Foodoodle I realize that my grouping of heroes of the revolution actually depicts the "First Family" of the revolution: Julia and James, the mother and father of America's gourmet food awakening, and Alice and Jeremiah, the feuding but brilliant siblings who merged their parents' Franco/American sensibilities into a new California/American cuisine.

The words used to describe a devotion to the pleasures of the table change in every era. The term I grew up with, "gourmet," is fading. In fact, it's so co-opted now, one is advised to steer clear of restaurants and food products labeled "gourmet." The ubiquitous "foodie" has, to a large extent, taken the place of gourmet, though I prefer more dignified terms like "foodist" and "culinarian" to describe my colleagues and myself. I do end up using foodie from time to time, usually in an ironic context, just as I open, on occasion, cans of commercial chicken and beef stock in my kitchen. It's convenient and does the trick, though I always feel a bit guilty.

I came up with the term "gastronaut" to describe gourmets of the 21st century, not imagining that it would become oddly appropriate in reference to the space-age cooking that would emerge with the Molecular Gastronomy movement out of Spain. More recently I coined the term "culineer" (as in culinary pioneer) to reference the young operators of those up-graded taco trucks, street food stands and "pop-up" restaurants that service a sustainably locavoracious customer base.

I like the term "foodiots," which I found recently on a blog, used to describe those who are compelled to share every detail of every meal they eat. But who knows which term will in the end define our food-obsessed era. I still cling to the retro terms gourmet, gourmand, gastronome and epicure, quaint references to a more innocent time (some would say a less conscious time) when cooking and eating were less about politics and survival than about art and pleasure.

This Foodoodle from 1990 was published in *Berkeley Insider* magazine in April 1993 along with my article — "A Fourth Street Grilling" — which explored a Michael Bauer pan in the *San Francisco Chronicle* some months earlier of Berkeley's Fourth Street Grill, which had recently reopened with a new menu and owner. I pitched my article to the *Insider* as a "review of a review," which I thought was a clever way to launch my tenure as the magazine's new restaurant and food editor. The idea was to explore the métier of the restaurant critic, which has always seemed mysterious to me, if not professionally problematic: Who gets to be a restaurant critic? What are the credentials, rules, and ethics for judging restaurants? I had attended a professional seminar on restaurant criticism that explored these issues, and thought Bauer's review — one of the most scathing I had ever read and, in my opinion,

exaggerated if not inaccurate regarding the Grill's obvious shortcomings — would be a good case study for applying my newly acquired reviewer perspectives. The new Fourth Street Grill didn't last much past Bauer's slam and my rebuttal in the *Insider*. Nor did my ambitions as a restaurant critic. The publisher/editor team at the *Insider*, Burt Dragin and Hank Resnik, shut the magazine down a year or so later. Although I was sorry to see the magazine go, along with my Berkeley-based vehicle for food writing, it was perhaps, for me, a blessing in disguise. Making and breaking restaurants (and careers) didn't really appeal to me. Unlike Mr. Bauer, I apparently didn't have the stomach for the job.

This analysis was based on two shopping bags filled with similar products, one with Safeway's standard (corporate, highly processed) versions and the other with Park and Shop's pricey up-scale (imported or local artisanal/organic) brands. The question then was whether the new up-scale version was worth twice the old, standard version, a legitimate consideration at the time, if not today.

I began thinking about meatballs, and their function as a carrier for global flavor, when I discovered Daniel Spoerri's remarkable text, "A Dissertation on Keftedes," in his 1970 book *The Mythological Travels* (Something Else Press). This was in 1972, just as I began work on my own garlic "dissertation."

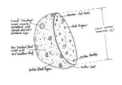

Spoerri, a renowned Swiss artist, had made his reputation in Europe as a member of the Fluxus group and the *Nouveaux Realistes*, both important post-WWII art movements. His interest in food as art material was obvious in his highly regarded "snare-picture" assemblages which included entire dinner tables with all their contents — the silverware, glasses and the plates with leftover food attached — mounted vertically on a wall. One of the most famous snare pieces featured the remains of a meal consumed by Marcel Duchamp which recently sold at auction for $250,000.

An obsessive fascination with food was also captured in the diary Spoerri kept during his stay on the remote Greek Island of Symi (the closest Greek island to the coast of Turkey) — "A Gastronomic Itinerary," also included in *The Mythological Travels*. I loved Spoerri's food texts, and, following my own visit to Symi, determined to re-issue the two food-related sections of *The Mythological Travels* in a new illustrated Aris Books edition. I contacted the maestro and arranged to publish the book in 1982 with a new title. I proposed *Mythology & Meatballs: A Greek Island Diary Cookbook*, which I thought captured the ironic spirit of Spoerri's work.

I have been told by Nach Waxman, the genial and veteran cookbook dealer/collector at Kitchen Arts & Letters in New York, that the book never sold well because of that title. This despite a fine review in *Newsweek* magazine: "It's a work to be savored in the reading...marvelously screwy... a Dadaist sampler of culinary oddments." It was perhaps not a very commercial title, but then Spoerri was not a commercial food writer.

And although Maestro Spoerri had approved the title, I nevertheless express apologies once again for the poor sales.

Spoerri lives today in Tuscany on the grounds of Il Giardino di Daniel Spoerri, an estate comprised of over 80 garden-art installations by Mr. Spoerri and artists from all over Europe. It's operated by a foundation and is open to the public.

Niloufer introduced the Gourmet Ghetto to the marvels of her native Bombay cuisine in the 1980's through her street food feasts at Chez Panisse and her cooking classes. When she rented the Aris Test Kitchen to give a series of classes on tropical cuisines, she included in one class a recipe for the date milk shakes she discovered at a food stand in the Southern California desert town of Indio, the "date capital of America," near Palm Springs. These very simple but exotic-tasting shakes are made by pureeing vanilla ice cream, pitted dates and milk. I must have missed the class and I didn't come across her date shakes until I read her 2008 cookbook, *My Bombay Kitchen*. I was fascinated because I had loved these very same shakes as a kid when my family passed through Indio while on Easter vacations in Palm Springs.

# 2003–2010

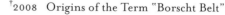

I've seen in cookware shops "tool belts" for chefs, but this belt was designed for finicky eaters. It should be noted that Toulouse-Lautrec always carried with him, as reported in the 1966 book, *The Art of Cuisine*, a piece of nutmeg and a little grater he used to flavor his port after meals in restaurants.

Chef Canales' annual "Whole Hog" dinners at Oliveto Restaurant are legendary, especially within the porcine community.

The upper bodies of Leonardo's apostle/chefs maintain the same symbolic and structural positions as in the original painting, but the lower halves of the characters on either side of the shortened Passover table/hospital bed had to be added, and I accept full artistic responsibility.

The Borscht Belt I grew up with was not in New York's Catskill Mountains where comedians like Henny Young- man and Milton Berle performed at Jewish resorts. My Borscht Belt was Boyle Heights, an area near downtown Los Angeles where a large population of immigrant Jews had settled. The "belt" extended west to the Fairfax Avenue district where Jewish delis and kosher shops still thrive.

As a kid, I assumed the area's name was "Boil Heights" in reference to the bland boiled foods my grandparents were eating at home — boiled beef, beef tongue and chicken. I didn't know that these dishes were just the poor relatives of Europe's great braises, boils and soups which I would learn to love during trips to Europe in the 1960's.

My respect for the "food of my fathers" grew as I got older, resulting by the 1990's in a personal comfort-food counter-revolution against what felt like my overly-precious and restrictive fancy-food fixation. I made the documentary, "Divine Food: One Hundred Years in the Kosher Delicates- sen Trade" with Bill Chayes in 1998 and began eating at Saul's Deli with a group of deli "mavens," right in the heart of the Gourmet Ghetto, an irony I explore elsewhere (see page 84). Saul's heroically blends Jewish taste memory and Gourmet Ghetto food standards, putting the lie to the prevail- ing notion that the Jewish deli is dead or dying. The American Jewish deli has been dying, and being reborn, for well over a century.

I'd like to think that James Beard went to the first Gilroy Garlic Festival in 1978 and visited the Lovers of the Stinking Rose booth. And if he had, I would have thanked him for his dish, Chicken with 40 Cloves of Garlic. His recipe for the Provençal classic was an inspiration to Berkeley's garlic subculture in the 1970's and to American cooks everywhere.

John Thorne has a great section in his book, *Outlaw Cook* (1992), on the origins of this dish claimed by several regions in Southern France. But it was Beard's version of the dish in his 1974 book *Beard on Food* that helped turn Americans on to the milder virtues of garlic when cooked slowly and long with moderate heat.

This kitchen staff line-up is based on the classic Brigade system, established by Georges Auguste Escoffier in the 19th century. I have modified some of the positions, or added new ones, based on popular dishes today never served in Escoffier's restaurants, such as pizza and BBQ, and kitchen functions not imagined then, such as the recycling of plastic and paper. I like the idea of custom toques reflecting each cooking position rather than the toque's complete elimination, as one notes in today's post-revolu- tionary restaurant scene. If the shoes make the man, doesn't the hat make the chef?

*For Jerry Budrick and Michale Perrella*

Golf is the perfect sport for chefs and their crews. The restaurant business is, for many who work in it, a nocturnal affair and one of the compensations is that staffers can recover the next day with hobbies and recreation before returning to the stoves and tables at night. Another advantage of golf over most sports is that it can be played, if not well, while drinking. After all, it was invented by Scotch drinkers.

Jerry Budrick, co-owner and uber-waiter at Chez Panisse in the 70's and 80's, and Michale Perrella, the founding pizza maker at the Chez Panisse Café, together initiated the Chez Panisse Golf Tournament at Berkeley's Tilden Park Golf Course in the early 1980's. The annual tournament ended after only a few years when a golf cart carrying Victoria Kroyer Wise, the first chef at Chez Panisse and the then-owner of Pig-by-the-Tail Charcuterie, careened around a tight corner on the first hole, throwing Ms. Wise out of the cart and breaking her leg. The facts of the incident are murky, so I don't know who was at fault and why. But rumor has it that either the cart driver (a busboy at the restaurant) was DUI, or Victoria was GUI (golfing under the influence), or both. Bottom line, the insurance company covering Tilden Park Golf Course said "No" to future Chez Panisse golf tournaments. More than the tournament itself, I miss the great outdoor BBQs we had at the park after the competition had ended and prizes for the winners were handed out.

Bob is one of several high school friends who came to the Bay Area with me from L.A. in the mid 60's. He briefly worked at

the Cheese Board in the late 60's, became a video artist in the 70's, then had a successful career in television as Executive Producer for KRON. By the 1990's Bob was working with wife Maggie Blyth Klein at their Oliveto Restaurant in Oakland. Every fall Bob voyages to Italy's Piemonte region to purchase the white truffles that will be featured at Oliveto's Truffle Festival in November. In early fall, the Bay Area's summer garlic celebrations are fading and hunger for truffles and other fungi, such as chanterelles, starts to build after the first rains. White truffles (Tuber magnatum) will break one's fixation on garlic (Allium sativum), at least during the peak of their short season. Chef Paul Canales' truffle-slathered pastas and meat braises can, in fact, reduce garlic's symphonic heft to mere background music. When the powerful Piemonte truffles go on the menu, you forget all about the charms of the humble Allium sativum, at least until the check arrives: Those luscious, fecund fungi Bob provides for Oliveto every year are, in fact, *molto costose!*

*In memory of Anzonini del Puerto, Butcher of Bulls*

Anzonini, a flamenco singer and professional butcher and sausage maker from the small town of Puerto in southern Spain, lived in Berkeley during the late 1970's with Pat Darrow. (See note on "Salvador Deli" for more on Pat, page 138.) The frequent "fiestas" at Pat's house were well attended by the Bay Area's flamenco crowd that worshipped Anzonini's singing and dancing, and by Berkeley's foodists who loved his cooking. His sausages were inspirational to many in the Ghetto, especially Bruce Aidells, and for a time were sold at Pig-by-the-Tail Charcuterie. (See page 91 for more on Anzonini.)

Italy's Slow Food movement logo, the snail, shared by America's offshoot organization, Slow Food USA, is itself a Foodoodle! One less food pun for me to play with, though there are crabs and turtles to consider.

The idea of the "dream kitchen," a subset of the "dream house," is almost certainly a creation of the home furnishings and remodeling industries in cahoots with appliance manufacturers. As home kitchens began the transition from servants' workspace to family room and great room after WWII, kitchen remodels became a status symbol for the increasingly affluent middle class.

My own quest for a dream kitchen took me to visit Monet's Giverny. I was as excited to see his kitchen, which I had drooled over in magazines and picture books, as the gardens he made famous in his paintings, especially the Water Lilies series. But my grand image of Monet's kitchen turned out to be more dream than reality. With all its gorgeous tiling, handsome vintage stoves and folksy painted cabinetry, it was just a moderate-sized haute bourgeois country kitchen of the period, not the to-die-for kitchen dream I imagined. Monet's kitchen, which he and his family seldom entered, was designed for the food that would be made there by his beloved cooks. (Monet was a serious and demanding gourmand.) Today, we do more living in our "live-in" and "eat-in" dream kitchens than cooking.

When my own dream kitchen was finally nearing completion, Paul Bertolli, then the executive chef at Oliveto, came to a party at my house and took a tour with me of the space. His first comment was, "Where's the wood-burning hearth?" For Bertolli, a kitchen without open-hearth cooking is not a dream kitchen at all.

For me, cooking over wood or charcoal is something you do outside in your *outdoor* dream kitchen. Which just goes to prove the point: One cook's dream kitchen is another's nightmare.

M.F.K. Fisher's book, *How To Cook a Wolf*, is a WWII-era treatise on economical eating during lean times when, she wrote, "the wolf is at the door." This Foodoodle merges Ms. Fisher's wolf with the brand name of a popular high-end kitchen range — the Wolf.

The Wolf Appliance Company, which merged a few years back with Sub-Zero Freezer Company, used to attach a cute, red, wolf ornament to its ranges, but has since discontinued its distinctive logo. That little smiling critter greeted me every time I walked into my kitchen and faced my vintage 1980 Wolf cook-top, and made me smile. Someone in the combined company's public relations (or legal) department must have made the assessment that Wolf 's wolf was no longer a politically or gastronomically correct marketing symbol given the endangered status of some wolf populations. Such a pity — for the wolves and the Wolf!

But with Ms. Fisher's "wolf" back at America's door, Wolf/Sub-Zero ought to consider a new line of economical ranges, with the happy red Wolf company ornament back where it belongs. A portion of the proceeds from the sale of the ranges could be donated to a wolf-preservation organization. I say, "Bring back the wolf!"

This Foodoodle was sketched in London in September 2008 after I had tea at the high-end Lanesborough Hotel, which boasts that its "tea sommelier" is the first in Great Britain. While the U.S. financial system was collapsing along with Great Britain's, a posh afternoon tea ritual set me back close to $400. I had no idea what the most expensive afternoon tea in London would cost, with all its bells and whistles, but I found out at the Lanesborough. Definitely the "highest" tea I've had, or will ever have.

Chefs become celebrities at their peril, or at least at their restaurant's peril. Paul Bocuse is the original poster boy for the chef-as-celebrity phenomenon, and apparently his restaurant is a sad reminder of its former glory.

Today's celebrity chefs include Britain's Gordan Ramsay. When Gordon yells at young, clueless chefs on his TV series "Ramsay's Kitchen Nightmares," I wonder if that's how he trains his own cooks. Based on the dried out pork I had at the pricey (and recently Michelin-demoted) Gordon Ramsay at Claridge's in London, I have to conclude that he didn't shout loud enough. The only truly delicious thing on the plate was the Calvados *jus* drizzled around the Suffolk pork, and it didn't go very far — the three tiny portions of belly, loin and cheek acted like little sponges sucking up the sauce after only a few bites.

And then there's former Iron Chef Mario Batali, whose restaurants appear to be still vibrant. But how long can that last when Don Batali and his Sancho Panza "Bittman" (food writer Mark Bittman) are dragging Gwyneth Paltrow and the Spanish starlet Claudia Bassols around Spain in sports cars on the PBS cooking/travel show in 2009, "Spain… on the road

Again"? The show was positively moronic. Maybe I'm just jealous — who wouldn't want to travel around Spain gorging on great food and scenery with gorgeous Paltrow and Bassols? But for my taste, the sycophantic banter (going in all directions) and negligible food content of this overblown tapas travelogue is an embarrassment for all concerned, including those gorgeous Mercedes convertibles.

The original collage from 1981 is missing, so I made a new collage (in color) and then a drawing from that. The "Piecasso" signature is a reproduction of what appeared in the 1981 issue of *Kajun Call*.

When a group from the Cheese Board, led by Pat Darrow, began planning a collectively-run café at the U.C. Berkeley Art Museum in 1971, we all began suggesting names. I put forth "Salvador Deli," which seemed totally appropriate for a casual museum café. Evidently Peter Selz, the director of the museum and a distinguished professor of art history, as well as several members of our own group, thought it too cute. Pat loved "Museum Eats," but that was considered too funky. "The Swallow" was the collective's conservative choice and it became a Berkeley icon for almost 20 years.

There was resistance at first to the idea of a café collective at the art museum, both from Professor Selz's bosses at the University, who didn't trust a business without a "boss," and from within the Cheese Board, too. Apparently the Cheese Board's crusty co-founder, Sahag Avedisian, didn't trust either U.C. Berkeley or Pat Darrow. But Pat, who was a passionate and talented cook with a vision, persevered, and The Swallow opened in 1972, next door to the museum's popular Pacific Film Archives.

The Swallow turned out to be a magnet for food talent, but curiously the workers that went on to bigger careers in food did so more with words than cooking: S. Irene Virbila (restaurant critic), Maggie Blyth Klein (author/restaurateur), the late Helen Gustafson (tea book author) and writer/editor Ruth Reichl, who wrote about her experiences at the café in her 1999 memoir, *Tender At the Bone*.

I have a vivid recollection of meeting Ruth at The Swallow, just as she was joining the collective in 1974 and I was phasing out. First, there was the hair — long, curly, jet black Medusa-like locks cascading down her back. Flirting would be useless, I quickly concluded — she was married. Hearing about my recently published *Book of Garlic*, Ruth told me that she had written a cookbook in 1972, *Mmmmm, A Feastiary*, published by Holt Rinehart in New York. Holt was the publisher that had just bought up the rights to my garlic book, which I had recently co-published with my childhood friend, the late poet, Dennis Koran, of Panjandrum Press in San Francisco. The new Holt edition would be published in 1975.

It was clear from that first encounter with Ruth that she had already put *Mmmmm* behind her, and that there would be no collaborative Holt/Swallow author promotions or national book tours. However, Ruth and I did collaborate some years later when she wrote an article on garlic for

*New West* magazine's "Food Fever" issue (May 1979). For that article we traveled together, along with Bruce Aidells and Les Blank, to visit the eccentric and charming French chef and restaurateur, Robert Charles, at his infamous garlic shrine, La Vieille Maison, in Truckee, California.

I recently ran into the still-vigorous Peter Selz while shopping at the Cheese Board, and I re-introduced myself to the Professor as a member of the first contingent at The Swallow café. He lit up and waved his hand towards several Cheese Boarders rolling out bread dough in the back of the store and exclaimed, "I still don't understand how a business without a boss can be so successful!"

This drawing of Bruce sniffing a garlic bulb and wearing the Lovers of the Stinking Rose ceremonial garlic toque (sewn by Linda Kirkhorn) based on the cover of the Summer 1979 issue of the *Garlic Times* newsletter.

For Maggie Blyth Klein

I met olive oil diva Maggie Blyth Klein at a "gourmet club" dinner party she hosted in 1970 at her house on Derby St. in South Berkeley. Maggie had an elegant way with food and was one of the best cooks in our growing circle of would-be gourmets. At The Swallow café she became, in addition to her creative role in the kitchen, the group's resident heart throb. Enigmatic, droll and shy, Maggie was irresistible, especially to the two Bobs in our crowd — Bob Waks and Bob Klein. Klein prevailed after a long courtship, and he and Maggie were married in 1973.

I was taken with Maggie too, albeit on a culinary/literary level. The story begins of course in the Gourmet Ghetto. I met a charming fellow outside Peet's in 1982, John Meis, who was coffee klatching that morning with my friend, the novelist Chester Aaron. Chester, by the way, would succeed me as "Mr. Garlic" with the exotic heirloom garlic varieties he grows on his Sonoma, California farm and his delightful books about his life with garlic published by Berkeley's Ten Speed Press in the 1990's.

John Meis mentioned to me that he had just been hired by an olive oil *frantoio* in Tuscany, Badia a Coltibuono, to help them introduce their high-end, peppery oil in the U.S. The idea for an Aris book on olive oil came out of that contact with John, and he agreed to help. Maggie was a perfect match for the project as she was, in addition to being a talented cook, a botanical illustrator and, after her stint at The Swallow, an editor for U.C. Berkeley's Agricultural Sciences Publications — all the right credentials for the author of *The Feast of the Olive*.

No one at Aris anticipated the splash Maggie's book would make when it arrived in 1983. At an olive oil tasting event at Dean & DeLuca in New York to celebrate the book's publication, members of New York's food elite showed up, including Florence Fabricant and Calvin Trillin. According to Isaac Cronin, Aris' first author (*The International Squid Cookbook*) and marketing director, the event — with hors d'oeuvres based on recipes from the book — was the first organized tasting of Extra Virgin Italian oils in the U.S. Maggie had arrived as America's Extra Virgin queen. Her Italian restaurant, Oliveto, arrived in Oakland three years later.

# BIBLIOGRAPHY

Bemelmans, Ludwig. *To The One I Love The Best.* New York: The Viking Press, 1955.

Bemelmans, Ludwig. *Hotel Bemelmans.* New York: Ebury Press, 1956.

Bourdain, Anthony. *Kitchen Confidential: Adventures in the Culinary Underbelly.* New York: The Echo Press, 2000.

Brillat-Savarin, Jean Anthelme, Fisher, M.F.K. trans. *The Physiology of Taste or Meditations on Transcendental Gastronomy.* New York: Alfred Knopf, 1979.

Cheese Board Collective. *The Cheese Board Collective Works.* Berkeley: Ten Speed Press, 2003.

Curnonsky. *Traditional Recipes of the Provinces of France.* New York: Doubleday & Company, 1961.

Courtine, Robert. *The Hundred Glories of French Cooking.* New York: Farrar, Straus and Giroux, 1973.

Dali, Salvador. *Les Diners de Gala.* New York: Felice, 1973.

David, Elizabeth. *French Provincial Cooking.* London: Michael Joseph, 1960.

David, Narsai; Muscatine, Doris. *Monday Night at Narsai's.* New York: Simon and Schuster, 1987.

Dutton, Denis. *The Art Instinct: Beauty, Pleasure, and Human Evolution.* New York: Bloomsbury Press, 2009.

Ellwanger, George. *The Pleasures of the Table: An Account of Gastronomy From Ancient Days to Present Times.* New York: Doubleday Page and Co., 1902.

Fisher, M.F.K. *An Alphabet for Gourmets.* New York: The Viking Press, 1949.

Freedman, Paul, ed. *Food: The History of Taste.* Berkeley: University of California Press, 2007.

Freudenheim, Leslie M. *Building with Nature: Inspiration for the Arts & Crafts Home.* Salt Lake City: Gibbs Smith, Publisher, 2005.

Gluck, Mary. *Popular Bohemia: Modernism and Urban Culture in Nineteenth-Century Paris.* Cambridge: Harvard University Press, 2005.

Hamilton, Richard and Todoli, Vicente, eds. *Food for thought, Thought for Food.* New York: Actar, 2009.

Harris, Lloyd J. *The Book of Garlic.* Berkeley: Aris Books, 1979.

Harris, L. John. *The Official Garlic Lovers Handbook.* Berkeley: Aris Books, 1986.

Herny, Ed; Rideout, Shelly; Wadell, Katie. *Berkeley Bohemia: Artists and Visionaries of the Early 20th Century.* Salt Lake City: Gibbs Smith, Publishers, 2008.

Kamp, David. *The United States of Arugula: How We Became a Gourmet Nation.* New York: Broadway Books, 2006.

Kato, Yoshio. *Garlic, The Unknown Miracle Worker: Odorless Garlic Medicine and Garlic Flow-Leben.* Amagasaki, Japan: Oyama Garlic Laboratory, 1973.

Keeler, Charles. *The Simple Home.* San Francisco: Paul Elder, 1904.

King, Niloufer Ichaporia. *My Bombay Kitchen: Traditional and Modern Parsi Home Cooking.* Berkeley: University of California Press, 2007.

Liebling, A. J. *Between Meals: An Appetite for Paris.* New York: North Point Press, 1986.

McNamee, Thomas. *Alice Waters and Chez Panisse.* New York: Penguin Books, 2007.

Michaels, Heide. *Monet's House: an Impressionist Interior.* London: Frances Lincoln, 1997.

Petrini, Carlo. *Slow Food Revolution: A New Culture for Eating and Living.* New York: Rizzoli, 2005.

Point, Fernand. *Ma Gastronomie.* Wilton: Lyceum Books, 1974.

Reed, Christopher. *Bloomsbury Rooms: Modernism, Subculture, and Domesticity.* New Haven: Yale University Press, 2004.

Revel, Jean-François. *Culture & Cuisine: A Journey Through the History of Food.* New York: Da Capo Press, 1982.

Ruhlman, Michael. *The Soul of a Chef: The Journey Toward Perfection.* New York: Viking, 2000.

Ruhlman, Michael. *The Reach of a Chef: Professional Cooks in the Age of Celebrity.* New York: Penguin Books, 2006.

Steinberger, Michael. *Au Revoir to All That: Food, Wine, and the End of France.* New York: Bloomsbury, 2009.

Strauss, Walter L., ed. *The Complete Engravings, Etchings and Drypoints of Albrecht Durer.* New York: Dover Publications, Inc.,1972.

Schwartz, Richard. *Eccentrics, Heroes, and Cutthroats of Old Berkeley.* Berkeley: RSB Books, 2007.

This, Herve. *Molecular Gastronomy: Exploring the Science of Flavor.* New York: Columbia University Press, 2002.

Thorne, John. *Outlaw Cook.* New York: Farrar, Straus and Giroux, 1992.

Toulouse-Lautrec, Henri de; Joyant, Maurice. *The Art of Cuisine.* New York: Crescent Books,1966.

Tower, Jeremiah. *California Dish: What I Saw (and Cooked) at the American Culinary Revolution.* New York: Free Press, 2003.

Waters, Alice. *The Art of Simple Food: Notes, Lessons, and Recipes From a Delicious Revolution.* New York: Clarkson Potter, 2007.

Weinstein, Dave. *It Came from Berkeley: How Berkeley Changed the World.* Salt Lake City: Gibbs Smith, Publishers, 2008.

Wise, Victoria. *American Charcuterie: Recipes From Pig-by-the-Tail.* New York: The Viking Press, 1986.

# ACKNOWLEDGEMENTS

*I* would like to express my gratitude to those who have supported my food doodling over the years and helped to bring a Foodoodle book into being. Peter Beren, Bay Area publishing consultant and agent, understood the idea from the very beginning and was a savvy advisor. Tom Farber of Berkeley's El León Literary Arts gave encouragement when I needed it.

Special thanks to Sharon Rudnick for her perceptive editing and steadfast encouragement. My designer, Peter Rinzler, approached the book with an artistic eye and detailed follow-through. Alex Harris drew the clever art frames for the book's cover and designed the Foodoodle website. Kit Duane, El León's editor, expertly proof read the book at the end.

Much appreciation to those who offered critical feedback on various drafts of the text: Michele Anna Jordan, Paul Terrell, Maggie Klein, Clair "Gus"Gustafson, Brad Bunnin, Nenelle Bunnin, Shana Sturm, Susan McConnell and Dave Weinstein.

I received professional advice, historical corrections and helpful comments from (in no special order): Victoria Kroyer Wise, Jerry Budrick, Tracy Johnston, Isaac Cronin, Eric Sartenaer, Les Blank, Marilyn Rinzler, Leonard Pitt, Charles Perry, Hank Resnik, S. Irene Virbila, Ed Behr, Jim Mellgren, Giorgia Neidorf, Marta Salas-Porros, Jim Melchert, Joyce Goldstein, David Cole, Sarah Schantz, Andy Ross, LeeAnn Sandefer Lyman, Stuart Marcus, Tony Dubovsky, Deborah Fabricant, Bruce Aidells, Peter Selz, Kaaren Kitchell, Hannah Love, Bob Klein, Laura Josephson and Michael Haimovitz.

Thanks to members of The Cheese Board Collective, past and present, for sharing their memories, especially Pat Darrow, Darryl Henriques, Elizabeth Valoma, Bob Waks and Steve Sutcher. To Saul's Mavens, who kept me laughing (and eating) while the book took shape: May your names be inscribed in the book of pastrami! Designers Andrea Young and Oksana Teicholz helped me to imagine what the book could look like early in the production process. And merci beaucoup to Andrea and Jacques Valerio for the use of their Paris apartment and book collection while I worked on the text of Foodoodles. The two Gregs at North Berkeley's Copy Central were great helps with scans and the book's many mock-ups.

M.F.K. Fisher supported the cartoons when I was just getting started and her memory has sustained me through the years.

Eternal gratitude to my children, Max and Alex Harris, for their always supportive and sometimes challenging counsel. And to Josephine MacMillan, whose unwavering enthusiasm, inspiration and loving partnership kept me going.

# ABOUT THE AUTHOR

*A* native of Los Angeles, California, L. John Harris studied art and creative writing at the University of California at Berkeley from 1965-1969. Through the 1970's, while working a variety of part-time jobs in some of Berkeley's notorious food shops and restaurants, he wrote articles for the *Los Angeles Free Press*, co-published how-to books with Panjandrum Press in San Franciso, and wrote *The Book of Garlic* under his *nom de l'ail*, Lloyd J. Harris (1974). As a garlic activist, his Lovers of the Stinking Rose garlic club and its *Garlic Times* newsletter inspired garlic festivals and theme restaurants from California to Washington state, Kentucky and New York. His second book, *The Official Garlic Lovers Handbook*, was published in 1986. In 1981, Harris founded Aris Books, a specialty cookbook imprint, and in 1988 launched his Foodoodle byline in several Bay Area magazines. After the sale of Aris in 1990, Harris shifted his focus to documentary film making. He wrote and co-produced "Divine Food: 100 Years in the Kosher Delicatessen Trade" in 1998, and in 2001 wrote and co-directed the Emmy-nominated PBS special "Los Romeros: The Royal Family of the Guitar." Since 2004, he has produced the popular Guitarrada programs at the San Francisco Conservatory of Music featuring world-class guitarists playing vintage classical and flamenco guitars from his personal collection. Mr. Harris spends his time between California and Paris, France and is currently at work on a graphic novel.